Business PLUS

Preparing for the workplace

Margaret Helliwell

TOEIC® is a registered trademark of Educational Testing Service (ETS). This publication is not endorsed or approved by ETS.

CAMBRIDGE UNIVERSITY PRESS

Student's Book **2**

UNIVERSITY PRESS

79 Anson Road, #06-04/06, Singapore 079906

Cambridge University Press is part of the University of Cambridge.

It furthers the University's mission by disseminating knowledge in the pursuit of education, learning and research at the highest international levels of excellence.

www.cambridge.org
Information on this title: www.cambridge.org/9781107637641

© Cambridge University Press 2014

This publication is in copyright. Subject to statutory exception and to the provisions of relevant collective licensing agreements, no reproduction of any part may take place without the written permission of Cambridge University Press.

First published 2014

Printed in Singapore by C.O.S. Printers Pte Ltd

ISBN 978-1-107-63764-1 paperback Student's Book 2
ISBN 978-1-107-63872-3 paperback Teacher's Manual 2

Additional resources for this publication at www.cambridge.org/businessplus

Cambridge University Press has no responsibility for the persistence or accuracy of URLs for external or third-party internet websites referred to in this publication, and does not guarantee that any content on such websites is, or will remain, accurate or appropriate. Information regarding prices, travel timetables, and other factual information given in this work is correct at the time of first printing but Cambridge University Press does not guarantee the accuracy of such information thereafter.

Acknowledgments

The author and publisher thank the many teachers in the Asian region whose invaluable insights helped revise and fine-tune *Business Plus*. We would like to mention the following in particular:

Professor Hyojin Chung, Dongguk University, South Korea

Da-Fu Huang, Southern Taiwan University of Science and Technology, Tainan, Taiwan

Hsiu-Hui Su, Chaoyang University of Technology, Taichung, Taiwan

Gideon Hockley-Hills, SEICO Inc., Osaka, Japan

Kelly Kimura, Soka University, Tokyo, Japan

Ms. Sirirat Poomprasart, University of the Thai Chamber of Commerce (UTCC), Bangkok, Thailand

The author's special thanks go out to Stuart Vinnie, Cambridge University Press Senior Development Manager, Asia, whose experience of teachers' needs and teaching situations throughout Asia helped to mold her materials to best match the reality in the classroom, and on the editorial side, Chris Caridia, for his good ideas and endless patience. Last but not least, Bob Culverhouse and Ann Jobson for hours of patient listening!

The author would also like to thank the following Cambridge University Press regional staff for their support and advice, without which this course would never have been possible: Nuntaporn Phromphruk, Panthipa Rojanasuworapong and Sura Suksingh (Thailand); Ron Kim and Seil Choi (South Korea); Tomomi Katsuki, John Letcher, and David Moser (Japan); Irene Yang (Taiwan).

Book and cover design by Designers Collective
Book layout by Transnet Pte Ltd
Illustrations by Albert Design House
Casting and audio production by Voice Over Asia Co., Ltd

Plan of the book

	Business situation	Grammar focus	Listening and speaking	Vocabulary focus
Before you begin *Page viii*				
Unit 1 **Welcome to our company** *Pages 1–8*	A visitor	1 Review of present tenses 2 *Wh-* questions	1 Commuting in Jakarta 2 Talking about the ideal workplace	1 Welcoming a visitor 2 Describing people, places, and things
Unit 2 **Business communication** *Pages 9–16*	Videoconferences	1 Verb + *-ing* after prepositions 2 Past tense of *can, must, have to*	Communicating at work Talking about communicating outside work	Computers and the Internet
TOEIC® practice *Pages 17–18*				
Unit 3 **Products and services** *Pages 19–26*	Describing products	1 Review of past simple 2 The passive	1 Describing services 2 Talking about how to learn a foreign language	1 Adjectives to describe products and services 2 ASEAN: countries, languages, and people
Unit 4 **Targeting the customer** *Pages 27–34*	Advertising	1 First conditional 2 Adverbs of manner	1 Radio commercials 2 Talking about advertising	1 Advertising words 2 Easily confused words (1)
TOEIC® practice *Pages 35–36*				
Unit 5 **Achievements** *Pages 37–44*	Presenting facts and figures	1 Present perfect 2 *Since* and *for*	1 Personal achievements 2 Talking about successful people	1 Graphs and charts 2 Presenting information

Reading	Culture focus	Business writing	Learning outcomes
			Students can . . .
An unusual workplace	The right time		<ul><li>welcome a visitor in a business situation.</li><li>use the present tenses.</li><li>ask questions with *wh-* words.</li><li>understand a conversation about commuting.</li><li>talk about the ideal workplace.</li><li>ask people to describe things.</li><li>understand a text about working on an oil rig.</li><li>understand different attitudes to time and punctuality.</li></ul>
Skype is here to stay		Messages	<ul><li>understand a conversation about videoconferences.</li><li>use the *-ing* form of the verb after prepositions.</li><li>use modal verbs in the past and to give advice.</li><li>talk about communicating at work and outside work.</li><li>talk about computers and the Internet.</li><li>understand a text about Skype.</li><li>write telephone and text messages.</li></ul>
Wearable technology	Stereotypes		<ul><li>understand someone describing a product.</li><li>talk and ask questions using the past simple.</li><li>understand and use the passive.</li><li>understand a conversation about products and services.</li><li>talk about how to learn a foreign language.</li><li>use different adjectives to describe products and services.</li><li>understand the names of ASEAN countries, languages, and people.</li><li>understand a text about wearable technology.</li><li>discuss stereotypes.</li></ul>
An advertising trend		Formal and informal language in emails	<ul><li>understand a conversation about advertising.</li><li>understand and use the first conditional.</li><li>use adverbs of manner to talk about how they do things.</li><li>understand commercials and talk about advertising.</li><li>understand and use advertising words.</li><li>use some easily confused words correctly.</li><li>understand a text about an advertising trend.</li><li>recognize formal and informal language in emails.</li></ul>
Successful Asian businesspeople	Hand signals		<ul><li>understand a presentation of sales figures.</li><li>use the present perfect with *for* and *since*.</li><li>understand and talk about successful people.</li><li>describe graphs and charts.</li><li>open and close a presentation and use connecting words.</li><li>understand a text about successful Asian businesspeople.</li><li>understand typical hand signals.</li></ul>

Plan of the book

	Business situation	Grammar focus	Listening and speaking	Vocabulary focus
Unit 6 **How would you like to pay?** *Pages 45–52*	Banks and their services	1 Verb + object + *to do* 2 Defining relative clauses	1 A company and its money 2 Role play situations in a bank.	1 Dealing with money 2 Foreign currencies
TOEIC® practice *Pages 53–54*				
Unit 7 **Future trends** *Pages 55–62*	Top jobs for the future	*Will* and *going to* future	1 The future of education? 2 Talking about future trends	1 Work and jobs 2 College and university
Unit 8 **When things go wrong** *Pages 63–70*	Dealing with a complaint	1 Second conditional 2 Adverbs that modify adjectives	1 Making complaints 2 Talking about making complaints	1 Complaints and apologies 2 Easily confused words (2)
TOEIC® practice *Pages 71–72*				
Unit 9 **Socializing** *Pages 73–80*	Networking	1 Reflexive pronouns and *each other* 2 Present perfect with *ever, yet, already*	1 Planning a social program 2 Talking about a social program for visitors to your company	1 Phrasal verbs 2 Polite phrases for socializing
Unit 10 **Next on the agenda** *Pages 81–88*	Organizing a meeting	1 *May* and *might* 2 Grammar quiz	1 Meeting styles 2 Talking about organizing a meeting	1 Prefixes 2 Vocabulary quiz
TOEIC® practice *Pages 89–90*				

Partner files *Pages 91–94*   **Irregular verbs** *Page 95*   **Transcripts** *Pages 96–115*

Reading	Culture focus	Business writing	Learning outcomes
			Students can . . .
Group buying		Report on a sales trip	<ul><li>understand conversations in a bank.</li><li>use verbs + object + *to do*.</li><li>use defining relative clauses.</li><li>understand an interview about a company and its money.</li><li>role-play situations in a bank.</li><li>use different words to talk about money.</li><li>talk about different currencies.</li><li>understand an article about group buying.</li><li>write a short sales report.</li></ul>
Tomorrow's cities	Names and titles		<ul><li>understand people talking about their future careers.</li><li>use *will* and *going to* to talk about the future.</li><li>understand and talk about future trends in education.</li><li>use words for different jobs.</li><li>talk about college and university.</li><li>understand an article about a city of the future.</li><li>use names and titles in business in different countries.</li></ul>
Solving problems with a smile		Responding to a complaint	<ul><li>understand a complaint and an apology.</li><li>understand and use second conditional.</li><li>use adverbs that modify adjectives.</li><li>understand a conversation and talk about making complaints.</li><li>deal with complaints.</li><li>use easily confused words correctly.</li><li>understand a text about strange complaints in a hotel.</li><li>reply to a complaint email.</li></ul>
Social or antisocial networks?	Gift taboos in Asia		<ul><li>introduce themselves and make business contacts.</li><li>use reflexive pronouns and *each other*.</li><li>use the present perfect with *ever*, *yet*, and *already*.</li><li>plan a social program for visitors to a company.</li><li>use phrasal verbs.</li><li>use polite phrases for socializing.</li><li>understand a text about communication technology.</li><li>understand and talk about gift taboos in Asian countries.</li></ul>
Meetings etiquette in Japan		Writing an agenda	<ul><li>understand plans for a meeting.</li><li>use *may*, *might* and *maybe*.</li><li>understand about meeting styles.</li><li>organize a meeting.</li><li>use prefixes to make opposites.</li><li>understand an article about etiquette at meetings.</li><li>write an agenda for a meeting.</li></ul>

Before you begin

Can you match the business situations in Units 1–10 with the photos? Then check the units.

1 **Welcome to our company**
  A visitor

2 **Business communication**
  Videoconferences

3 **Products and services**
  Describing products

4 **Targeting the customer**
  Advertising

5 **Achievements**
  Presenting facts and figures

6 **How would you like to pay?**
  Banks and their services

7 **Future trends**
  Top jobs for the future

8 **When things go wrong**
  Dealing with a complaint

9 **Socializing**
  Networking

10 **Next on the agenda**
  Organizing a meeting

Welcome to our company

Unit 1

1 Business situation
A visitor

A 🔊 1 David Tan from Singapore is visiting Le Thi Mai and Tran Thanh Ly at their office in Hanoi. Listen to their conversation. Who says what? Write *M* for Mai, *L* for Ly, or *D* for David.

1 Welcome to our company. ....
2 It's great to see you again. ....
3 Pleased to meet you. ....
4 Our office is on the third floor. ....
5 Please, have a seat. ....
6 How do you take your tea? ....
7 What's the place like? ....
8 Could you tell me where the restroom is? ....
9 I'll be right back. ....
10 What's the plan for the day? ....

B Work with a partner. Student A is at work. Student B is a visitor.

Student A	Student B
Greet the visitor. You have met before. →	Greet A. You have met before.
Offer B a seat.	Thank A. Say something about the office.
Offer B tea or coffee. How does he or she take it?	Tell A tea or coffee and how you take it. Ask about the plan for the day.
Tell B about the plan for the day (meet colleagues – have meeting – lunch).	Tell A what you think of the plan. Ask the way to the restroom.
Tell B the way to the restroom. →	Thank A.

▷ • sales conference • enormous
• work on sth. • project • to share

I can welcome a visitor in a business situation.

2 Grammar focus
Focus 1: Review of present tenses

A Look at the sentences 1 to 3 from the conversation in 1A. Match them with the definitions A to C.

1 We're working on a project together. ....
2 We're meeting him at 11 o'clock. ....
3 Ly works with me in the sales department. ....

A the present simple to talk about something that happens usually or often
B the present continuous to talk about something that is happening now
C the present continuous to talk about a future plan

B Answer the questions. Use one of the present tenses.

1 What do you do every day?
2 What are you doing now?
3 What are you doing tomorrow?

> We don't use some verbs in the present continuous, for example *like, know, want, need, prefer, understand*:
> Now Mai <u>wants</u> to show David her office.
> Ly <u>understands</u> the questions now.

C Complete each sentence with a verb from the box in the correct present tense.

| attend | do | know | make | speak |
| understand | visit | wear (2x) | work (2x) | |

1 My boss .... (not) the conference tomorrow.
2 I .... a cup of tea. Would you like one?
3 Now I .... his telephone number.
4 How many guests .... the company this week?
5 Stop! You .... too fast. I .... (not).
6 What .... you usually .... in your free time?
7 Next month we .... on a project together.
8 I .... (not) glasses all the time, but I .... them now because I .... on the computer.

The glasses suit you.

D Match the two sentence halves.

1 Tom is not working right now   E
2 Huang doesn't work now   ....
3 Irfan writes a report   ....
4 Haziq is writing a report   ....
5 Robert comes from London   ....
6 David is coming from his hotel   ....

A because he's too old.
B and he lives there with his family.
C and will arrive soon.
D every time he attends a meeting.
E ~~because he's tired~~.
F about the meeting he had yesterday.

Tom is not working right now because he's tired.

▷ • glasses • report

I can use the present tenses.

Unit 1

2 Grammar focus
Focus 2: *Wh*-questions

E Look at these questions from the conversation in 1A and underline the questions words.

1 Where are you staying?
2 What's the plan for the day?
3 Who's that?
4 When are you having lunch?
5 Why not?

F Which question word asks about . . .

1 a time? ....
2 a person? ....
3 a thing? ....
4 a place? ....
5 a reason? ....

G Four visitors are waiting in your company's reception area. Look at their business cards and the schedule for the day. With a partner, ask and answer questions about them. Ask five questions about each person.

Who is Lam Ji Chiew? — He's . . .
Where does he work?

Schedule	Time	Visitor	Purpose of visit
May 23	09:00	Lam Ji Chiew	meeting with Ms. Wang
	09:00	Ken Clark	meeting with Mr. Zhao
	09:15	Ann Johnson	job interview with Mr. Zhang
	09:15	Kaito Sasaki	meeting with Mr. Yang

▷ ■ reception ■ schedule
  ■ job interview

I can use *wh*-words to ask questions.

3 Listening and speaking
Commuting in Jakarta

A Oliver Holliday started his new job in Jakarta today. It's the first day in his job. Over lunch he talks to Dian Natsir, a colleague, about commuting in Indonesia's capital. Before you listen, match words 1 to 6 with definitions A to F.

1 vehicle	....	A	make better
2 bus lane	....	B	a part of a town that is not close to the center
3 honk	....	C	bus, car, truck, bicycle, etc.
4 commute	....	D	part of a road only for buses
5 suburb	....	E	traveling from home to work and back
6 improve	....	F	the sound of a vehicle's horn

B 🎧 2 Now listen to the conversation and complete the sentences.
1 Oliver's journey to the office took .... hours.
2 About .... cars, motorcycles, and other vehicles are on the streets of Jakarta every day.
3 During Ramadan, workers are allowed to leave their jobs between ....
4 Sometimes the center of Jakarta is like one .... parking lot.
5 In the monsoon season, the .... makes things worse.
6 Dian lives in the .... of Jakarta, and it takes her about .... to get to work.
7 Dian usually has to stand on the bus because ....
8 The ticket collector on Dian's bus jumped off to ....

C Talking about ... the ideal workplace

Step 1: Think about your ideal workplace. Make notes about:

type of company	commute to work	colleagues	vacation time
location of company	type of office	hours	

Step 2: Interview another student about his/her ideal workplace. Are your ideas the same or different?

I would like / prefer . . . because . . .   *I wouldn't like / couldn't stand . . .*

Step 3: Tell the class which of your and your partner's ideas are the same and which are different.

My partner and I both agree that . . .
My partner thinks . . . , but I don't agree. I would prefer . . . because . . .

▷ ▪ to commute ▪ traffic jam
  ▪ suburbs ▪ public transportation

I can talk about my ideal workplace.

4 Vocabulary focus
Focus 1: Welcoming a visitor

A **1** Find ten words from the conversation in 1A in the box below. Then complete the sentences.

A	P	B	E	C	I	D	O	U	W	A	Y	E	R
F	R	G	C	H	A	H	I	J	E	K	L	M	E
C	O	M	F	O	R	T	A	B	L	E	N	S	S
E	J	B	O	W	A	B	C	D	C	H	I	O	T
B	E	Y	C	U	V	W	F	L	O	O	R	T	R
C	C	W	A	B	U	T	O	R	M	I	F	A	O
D	T	V	T	P	L	E	A	S	E	D	T	B	O
I	O	U	R	P	N	I	S	E	Y	Z	E	C	M
F	N	T	E	T	K	U	H	A	D	D	D	Y	Z
G	P	S	S	P	A	B	S	T	A	Y	I	N	G
K	Q	D	T	U	O	G	T	H	O	F	L	D	Y

1 My name is Tran Thanh Ly. .... to our company.
2 .... to meet you.
3 My office is on the second ....
4 Please, come this ....
5 Please, have a ....
6 .... do you take your tea?
7 Where are you .... ?
8 We're working on a .... together.
9 The hotel is very ....
10 Could you tell me where the .... is, please?

B Look at the phrases. Write *I* for the phrases you would say to a visitor to your company. Write *V* for the phrases the visitor would say to you.

1 Good morning. Can I help you?   I
2 I have an appointment with Ms. Wang.   V
3 Can I take your coat?   ....
4 I think Ms. Wang is expecting me.   ....
5 I'm sorry I'm a bit late.   ....
6 Please have a seat.   ....
7 Would you like something to drink?   ....
8 What's your hotel like?   ....

C Choose the correct preposition to complete the sentences.

| about   at (2x)   in   on (2x)   around   to |

1 Welcome .... our company.
2 Mai has told me a lot .... you.
3 We met .... the sales conference.
4 We are working .... a project together.
5 I'll be back .... a moment.
6 The restroom is .... the left.
7 We're meeting the sales manager .... 11 o'clock.
8 I'll show you .... the building.

Unit 1 | 5

4 Vocabulary focus
Focus 2: Describing people, places, and things

D Look at these questions and answers and complete the rule below.

What's the place like? – It's simple but very comfortable.
What's it like during Ramadan? – It's chaotic.
What's your commute like? – It's long and stressful.

We use *what + to be + subject + ...*
to ask about people, places, and things.

Note the difference:
What is your boss like?
– He's very nice.
How is your boss?
– Oh, he was sick, but now he's much better.

E Match the questions with the answers.

1 What are your colleagues like? **F**
2 What was the traffic like this morning? ....
3 What is your boss like? ....
4 What was the movie like? ....
5 What were the people at the party like? ....
6 What was the weather like during your vacation? ....

A Not as chaotic as it was yesterday.
B Noisy and funny. We had a great time.
C It was great. I love that director.
D Good. I really like working for him.
E Awful. It rained a lot.
F ~~They're very polite and friendly.~~

F Ask a partner about these things. Use *What ... like?*

1 his/her college
2 the town where he/she lives
3 his/her neighbors
4 the last movie he/she saw

G We can also use these phrases to ask about things. Choose one of the phrases to complete the questions.

What kind of . . .   What size . . .   What color . . .   What brand of . . .

1 clothes do you wear at work/college?
2 coffee do you drink?
3 emails do you write (in the office)?
4 magazines do you read?
5 smartphone do you prefer?
6 spreadsheet software do you use?
7 sports shoes do you wear?
8 food do you eat at lunchtime?

H Work with a partner. Take turns to ask and answer the questions in 4G.

I ▶ **Key words** Look at the words at the bottom of pages 1–4. Choose the best word to complete the sentences.

1 We got stuck in a .... on the way to work.
2 I went for a .... but I didn't get the job.
3 I don't have my own office. I .... one with a colleague.
4 Buses, trains, and the subway are part of the .... system.
5 Dian .... by bus to work every day.
6 .... means "really big."
7 I don't know if I have time. I'll have to check my ....
8 Mai and David met at a ....

I can ask people to describe things.

5 Reading
An unusual workplace

A) Before you read Skim the article and find out what Krisada Atthakor does in his free time.

Asian Business **Online**
looks at life and work on an offshore oil rig.

Krisada Atthakor is an engineer, and he loves his job! He is one of 340 people who live and work on an oil rig in the Gulf of Thailand. Space is limited – he shares his 16-by-16 meter bedroom with another engineer – but he isn't complaining. "Life is very comfortable on the rig," he says. "We don't have to do our own cleaning or cooking. Our cafeteria serves the most marvelous food from early in the morning until late at night."

Located 200 kilometers offshore, the rig pumps natural oil and gas from under the sea and stores it before it goes to customers on shore. After Krisada graduated from Bangkok Technical College, he attended a special training course for work on the oil rig. Now he says there is nowhere he would rather work. "Life is never boring at sea," he told Asian Business Online. "We work long shifts, sometimes up to 12 hours, but after work there's a movie theater and a gym where we can work out. And to relax I watch the sharks, sea turtles, and different kinds of fish that swim under and around the rig."

In the past, distance from friends and family was a problem for people who worked offshore, but since the introduction of fiber optics, there is now a good Internet connection, so everyone can enjoy Skyping and social networking.

"Another advantage of my workplace," says Krisada, "is that I never get stuck in traffic on the way to my job. I just jump out of bed, cross the deck, and I'm at work!"

B) Scanning for detail Are the statements correct? If not, correct them.
1. Krisada has his own room on the oil rig.
2. The workers have to clean their own rooms.
3. Krisada trained to work on the oil rig while he was at technical college.
4. Krisada sometimes gets bored on the oil rig.
5. It is impossible to work out when you live on the oil rig.
6. The sharks around the oil rig make Krisada feel nervous.
7. It is no longer a problem for workers on the oil rig to keep in touch with their families.

C) Now you Would you like to work on an offshore oil rig? Discuss in class. Think about these things:

| comfortable life | good food | movie theater | work out | no traffic jams |
| boring | long shifts | hard work | miss family and friends |

I can understand a text about working on an oil rig.

6 Culture focus
The right time

A Read about time and punctuality in business in different parts of the world. In which country . . .

1 do they expect to start and finish meetings punctually? ....
2 is it impolite to be the first person to leave a meeting? ....
3 are they flexible with time in private but not in business? ....
4 do they often blame the traffic when they are late? ....
5 should you never arrive earlier than the given time? ....
6 is it acceptable to arrive earlier than the given time? ....
7 is it normal to be late for a meeting? ....
8 do they not take deadlines seriously? ....

INDONESIA "Jam karet" means "rubber time," which means people can be flexible with time. Deadlines are not always taken seriously. If you want a meeting to begin at 9:30, it's best to invite for 9:00 – and don't get too upset if some people still show up at 9:45!

JAPAN Both in business and in private life, Japanese people often arrive early. The Japanese are very punctual about arriving at work as well as about starting meetings, but not about finishing them. Meetings often go on until a senior person decides the meeting is over. It might seem impolite to the group if you are the first person to leave.

MALAYSIA People generally are not very punctual. It is normal to be late for a meeting or appointment. The usual excuse is the traffic jams. Kuala Lumpur is a big city, and there are always traffic problems.

NORTHERN EUROPE Northern Europeans are usually very punctual, both in business and in private activities. Especially in Germany and Finland, it is important to be on time. Germans expect meetings to start on time, but they also expect them to finish on time.

SOUTHERN EUROPE People in southern European countries such as Spain and Italy are more relaxed about punctuality than Northern Europeans. But even here in business it is unacceptable to keep people waiting for more than 20 minutes.

THE PHILIPPINES It is common for private activities not to start on time. In fact, it is impolite to arrive at social events exactly on time. You are still on time if you come an hour late. But it is different in business, where punctuality makes a good impression.

B Now listen to these five businesspeople. Complete the sentences about what each person did wrong, why it was wrong, and why it happened.

1 Isamu Takahashi from Japan *arrived* for an appointment with his German teacher. It was wrong because the Germans .... In Japan people often ....
2 Katja Falkenberg from Germany wanted to .... a meeting with Japanese businesspeople because she had to .... It was wrong because in Japan ....
3 Nick Brown from England was .... for a meeting with an Italian customer. It was wrong because in Southern Europe it is ....
4 Her Filipino colleagues told Anina Fisk from Finland that their party would start at ...., so she arrived .... It was wrong because ....
5 When Philipp de Woolf from the Netherlands worked in Indonesia, he called a meeting for nine-thirty one morning, but .... Philipp was angry, but that was wrong because ....

Business communication

Unit 2

1 Business situation
Videoconferences

A 🔊 4 Sakura Kondo from Japan and Akmal Hashim from Malaysia work for a small British company in Kuala Lumpur. They are talking about videoconferences. Check (✔) the advantages and disadvantages they talk about.

Videoconferences			
Advantages		**Disadvantages**	
easy to keep in touch with business partners	☐	some people are shy in front of a camera	☐
saves time	☐	the equipment is expensive	☐
saves money	☐	no personal contact	☐
less traveling	☐	no time for small talk	☐
more people can take part	☐	different time zones	☐
better for the environment	☐	technical problems	☐

B 🔊 4 Listen to the conversation again and complete the sentences.

1 They had to stop the last videoconference because they . . .
2 Akmal thinks that business is about . . .
3 Sakura thinks you would need a lot of time to . . .
4 Akmal looks forward to . . .
5 Akmal is shy . . .
6 Akmal hopes that Sakura can give him . . .

▷ ▪ advantages ▪ disadvantages
  ▪ screen ▪ to interrupt

I can understand a conversation about videoconferences.

2 Grammar focus

Focus 1: Verb+-ing after prepositions

A 🔊 4 Listen to the conversation in 1A again. Add the missing prepositions.

	Preposition	Verb	
I'm responsible	....	setting up	the equipment.
Business is	....	building	personal relationships.
Think of the cost	....	getting	there.
I look forward	....	meeting	my contacts personally.
I'm fed up	....	traveling	around the world.
I'm pretty good	....	talking	to a camera.

Talking to a camera

B Complete the rule.

When a verb follows a preposition, the verb ends in ....

C Complete the sentences with the prepositions and the verb in the correct form.

about   at   for (2x)   instead of   of   to

1 I look forward .... (meet) my clients personally.
2 Shall we meet personally .... (talk) on the phone?
3 Excuse me .... (be) late for the meeting.
4 What about the cost .... (buy) the hardware?
5 The conference will be .... (improve) sales.
6 Skype is perfect .... (keep) in touch with clients.
7 Akmal is not good .... (talk) to a camera.

We're fed up with having technical problems.

D Make sentences with *by* + verb+-*ing*.

1	~~You can find a lot of information~~		A	(study) hard.
2	You can pass your exams		B	(look) it up in the dictionary.
3	You can remember what the teacher said	by	C	(take) notes.
4	You can find out what a word means		D	(check) your answers.
5	You can get better grades		E	~~(use) a search engine.~~

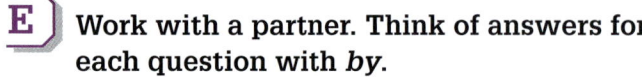

You can find a lot of information by using a search engine.

E Work with a partner. Think of answers for each question with *by*.

1 How can you improve your English?
  You can improve your English by . . .
2 How can you get fit?
3 How can you help to save the environment?

We use *by* and verb+-*ing* to say how something happens:

You can save the cost of flights by <u>having</u> a videoconference.

▷ • fed up • environment

I can use the -ing form of the verb after prepositions.

2 Grammar focus
Focus 2: The past tense of *can, must, have to*

F Read these parts of the conversation from 1A and put the underlined words in the chart.

Sakura: Hi, Akmal. Are you coming to the videoconference this afternoon?
Akmal: I <u>have to</u> be there, Sakura. I'm responsible for setting up the equipment, and I'm a bit nervous about it. Remember the last time we had a videoconference? We <u>had to</u> stop because of technical problems – we <u>couldn't</u> get a picture on the screen.
Sakura: Yes, I remember. I <u>can</u> see why you're nervous.

Present	Past
have to / must	
can	

We had to stop.

G Complete the second sentence in the past tense.
1 Every day, I have to get up early for work. Yesterday, I *had to get up early*.
2 Akio has to run for the bus every morning. Yesterday morning, he ....
3 I can't attend the meeting this week. Last week, I ....
4 We have to discuss some problems with our boss this afternoon. Last Friday, we
   ....
5 Can you contact your clients via Skype? .... yesterday?

H Complete the sentences with *can, can't, could,* or *couldn't* and one of the verbs.

| <s>attend</s> buy drive find get sleep speak wait |

1 I'm afraid I *can't attend* the meeting next week.
2 Akmal is so nervous about the videoconference, he .... at night.
3 We wanted to go to the concert, but we .... tickets.
4 Borin ...., but he doesn't have a car.
5 Ly .... her car keys, so she took the bus.
6 We .... anything because the shops were closed.
7 **A:** I'm sorry, I'm not ready yet.
   B: That's OK. I ....
8 Huang .... English when he was only five years old.

Huang

I Work with a partner.

Student A: Go to Partner file 1.
Student B: Look at the statements below. Your partner has four different statements. Take turns to read the statements and give each other advice. Use *should* or *shouldn't*.
1 "I need to have a meeting in Hanoi, but I don't have time to go there."
2 "I feel shy when I have to talk to a camera."
3 "I'm putting on weight."
4 "I'd like to meet some new people."

Should is not as strong as *must* and *have to*. We use it to give advice:

You look tired. You <u>should</u> go to bed earlier. You <u>shouldn't</u> work so hard.

I can use *can, must,* and *have to* in the past and *should* to give advice.

3 Listening and speaking
Communicating at work

A 🔊 5 Yi Ling Sim is taking part in a survey about how people communicate at work. Listen and check (✔) her answers. Sometimes more than one answer is correct.

COMMUNICATION AT WORK

1. How long do you spend online at work each day on average?
   - ☐ A less than two hours
   - ☐ B between two and four hours
   - ☐ C more than four hours

2. What is the main reason you go online at work?
   - ☐ A reading and writing emails
   - ☐ B Skyping
   - ☐ C researching on the Internet

3. How many emails do you send and receive each day at work?
   - ☐ A less than 10
   - ☐ B between 10 and 25
   - ☐ C more than 25

4. What sort of social media do you use in your company?
   - ☐ A chat rooms
   - ☐ B forums
   - ☐ C blogs

5. Which social networking sites do you use at work?
   - ☐ A none
   - ☐ B Twitter
   - ☐ C LinkedIn

6. How do you like to communicate?
   - ☐ A face-to-face
   - ☐ B on the phone
   - ☐ C via email

7. Do you ever communicate with handwritten messages?
   - ☐ A often
   - ☐ B sometimes
   - ☐ C never

8. How often do people in your office have videoconferences?
   - ☐ A often
   - ☐ B never
   - ☐ C sometimes

9. How often do people in your office have conference calls?
   - ☐ A often
   - ☐ B never
   - ☐ C sometimes

B Talking about ... communicating outside work

Step 1: Work with a partner. Make a questionnaire like the one in A about communication in your free time. Write at least six questions.

Example:
How long do you spend online at home every day on average?
- ☐ A less than one hour
- ☐ B between one and two hours
- ☐ C more than . . .

Step 2: Work in groups. Use your questionnaires to make a survey of your group's communication habits. Make notes.

Step 3: Tell the class what you found out about the habits of your group.

Most people in our group spend between one and two hours a day online. The main reason we go online is . . .

▷ • survey • to research
  • dozen • minutes

I can talk about communicating at work and outside work.

4 Vocabulary focus
Computers and the Internet

A Label the pictures with the numbers 1 to 10.

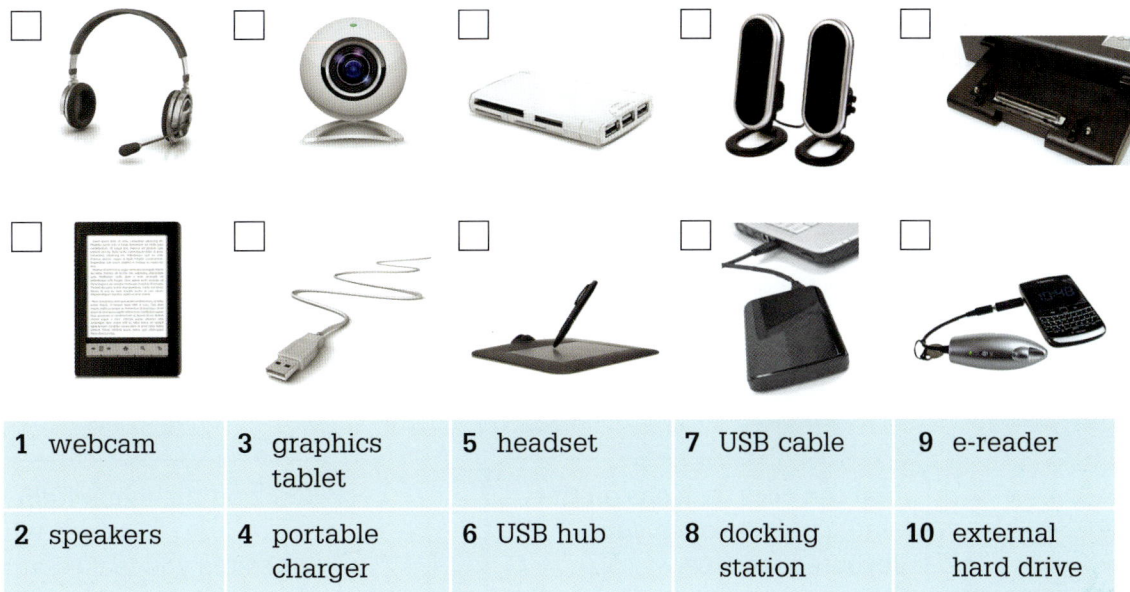

1	webcam	3	graphics tablet	5	headset	7	USB cable	9	e-reader
2	speakers	4	portable charger	6	USB hub	8	docking station	10	external hard drive

B Match the verbs 1 to 10 with the phrases A to J.

1	rename	....	A	changes
2	browse	....	B	a password
3	drag	....	C	a Wi-Fi signal
4	click	....	D	the Web
5	reset	....	E	the shift key
6	put	....	F	the computer
7	receive	....	G	on an icon
8	press	....	H	a file
9	restart	....	I	to the trash can
10	track	....	J	on standby

C Complete the sentences. Use verbs and phrases from 4B.

1 Before you shut down your computer, you should .... to save your work.
2 If you want to write in capital letters, you have to .... first.
3 For security reasons, you should .... now and then.
4 If you don't want to keep a file, you can .... it ....
5 In some places you can't ...., so you can't go online.
6 If you have a problem, it often helps to ....

D Work with a partner. Take turns to ask and answer the questions.

1 How do you shut down your computer?
2 What do you do if your Wi-Fi connection doesn't work?
3 When is it useful to track changes in a text?
4 How do you rename a file?
5 Do you usually shut your computer down or put it on standby? Why?

I can take telephone messages.

E Complete the comments about using the Internet with words from the box.

bookmarks   drop-down   history   links   scroll
tab   toolbar   zoom

1 There's a lot of information, so you need to .... down to find what you need.

2 There are a lot of useful .... to other websites.

3 You can click on icons on the .... to open your favorite websites.

4 To open a new .... click on the "+" above the tool bars.

5 There are some useful .... menus where you click on an arrow and a list appears.

6 I want to go back to the site, so I have added it to my ....

7 Click on the menu item "...................." to see which websites you looked at before.

8 If the font is too small, use control and "+" on the keyboard to .... in.

F Work with a partner. Look at the headings below on a company website.

| About us | Our staff | Our products and services | Careers | Contact us |

Where would you find information about . . .

1 addresses and phone number of the company?   ....
2 job opportunities?   ....
3 a description of the company?   ....
4 the people who work for the company?   ....
5 what the company offers?   ....

G ▶ **Key words** Look at the words at the bottom of pages 9–12. Choose the best words to complete the sentences.

1 Excuse me for ...., but I don't agree.
2 My job has .... and ....
3 Asian Business Online did a .... of people's communication habits.
4 They asked me to write the .... of the videoconference.
5 I prefer to watch movies on a big .... That's why I like the movie theater.
6 You can .... a lot of topics on the Internet.
7 "A ...." is the same as "twelve."
8 I'm .... with my job. I want to change it.

I can talk about computers and the Internet.

5 Reading
Skype is here to stay

A | Before you read Do you use Skype? How often? Who do you talk to?

Asian Business **Online**
looks at Skype's past successes and future developments.

Le Dinh Tung left Ho Chi Minh City six months ago to work in Sweden. He was not worried about keeping in touch with business partners, relatives, and friends back home because he was already a great fan of Skype. "Skype not only makes work easier, it also makes it possible for me to talk to my friends and family when I want to," he told Asian Business Online.

The Internet message service Skype has made the world smaller since it first appeared in 2003. At a time when people travel the world more and more, Skype brings people together. Users can make free calls to each other anywhere in the world, and the high sound and video quality gives them the feeling that they are in a room with the people they are talking to. This is what is so attractive about Skype, and today over 300 million users make two billion minutes of calls a day.

And Skype is not only for humans. At Cameron Park Zoo in Texas, in the United States, orangutans are given tasks. If they complete them, they get a reward: they are allowed to use Skype to talk to orangutans in other zoos!

Tung, who is himself an IT expert, says: "I think Skype is here to stay. We'll use it in more and more devices, such as videophones. I can imagine a time when you have a tablet in your kitchen, an Xbox connected in your living room, and you can be on a video call and it will follow you around the house. I think that time is not far away."

B | Scanning for detail What do these numbers refer to?

6   2003   300 million   2 billion

C | Comprehension

1. Where does Le Dinh Tung work?
2. Who does he talk to on Skype?
3. What is so attractive about Skype?
4. What is the orangutans' reward when they complete a task?
5. Tung says, "Skype is here to stay!" What does he mean?

D | Vocabulary in context Find words in the text that mean:

1. unhappy, thinking about problems
2. in contact
3. father, mother, sister, brother
4. a person who likes and admires something
5. a person who knows a lot about something
6. a piece of equipment
7. a place at home where you can sit and relax

I can understand a text about Skype.

6 Business writing
Messages

A 🎧 6 Listen to two telephone conversations between a secretary and two different callers. Below are the messages the secretary wrote down. There are three mistakes in each message. Correct the mistakes.

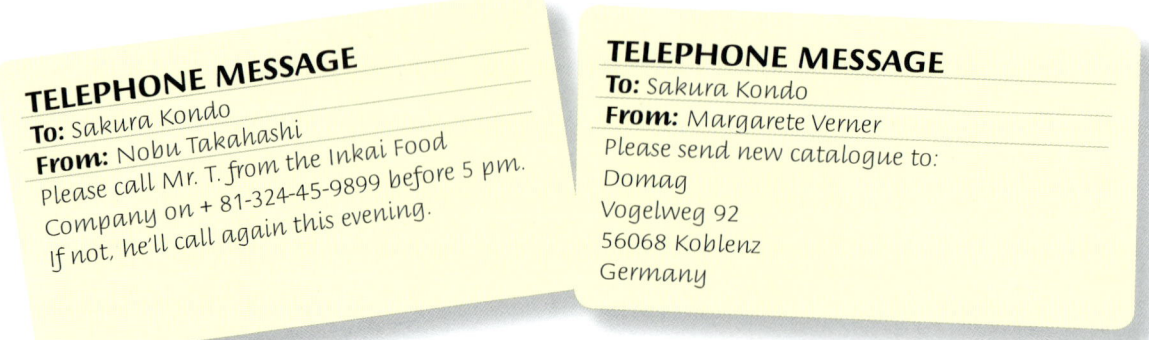

B 🎧 7 You work for an American company. Your boss, Ethan Lane, is away on a business trip. Listen to the voicemails, then complete your text messages for him. Write only the important information.

Message 1

Mr. Kowalski is in ....
until Friday. Please call today at
the ....
Tel: 065 8246 ....
Room number 1 ....

Message 2

Hendrik Edegran called from
.... He got
.... from John Fox.
He wants to know the name of
.... Please send email to
....

Message 3

.... called about
.... She can't
.... because
....
She'll call again to ....

Message 4

.... called. You met him
at .... in ....
He has checked ....
In January ....
but .... If you
have questions, call him at ....

C Can you understand these text messages?

1. WL B L8 4 MTG 2nite. *Will be late for meeting tonight.*
2. THX 4 YR MSG ....
3. WL C U L8 2nite ....
4. GD MTG? PCM ASAP. ....
5. WL U B at MTG 2morrow? ....

D Work with a partner. Write him or her a message in text message language. Your partner reads out the message.

TOEIC® practice

1 Listening

A 🔊 **Photographs** Listen. Then choose the sentence that best describes the photograph.

1 A ☐ B ☐ C ☐ D ☐   2 A ☐ B ☐ C ☐ D ☐

B 🔊 **Question-Response** Listen carefully. Choose the best response to the sentence you hear.

Example: When was your last vacation?
A ☑ Last May.   B ☐ Next week.   C ☐ In London.

1 A ☐ B ☐ C ☐   3 A ☐ B ☐ C ☐
2 A ☐ B ☐ C ☐   4 A ☐ B ☐ C ☐

2 Speaking

A **Describe a picture** Choose one of the pictures in 1A. Look at it for 30 seconds, then describe it in your own words.

B **Read a text aloud** You have 45 seconds to look at the text below. Then you have 45 seconds to read it aloud.

> The first Internet café or cybercafé was opened in Seoul in South Korea in March 1988 – two or three years before the first Internet café in the Western world. It was called the Electronic Café. Traditionally cafés are places where people meet, drink coffee, chat, read newspapers, and play games. The idea of an Internet café was to offer all these things, but also to offer Internet access. Internet cafés soon became very popular. But today many people have their own Internet connection prat home or on their laptops and smartphones using Wi-Fi, so perhaps the days of Internet cafés are over.

3 Reading

Incomplete sentences Choose the best word(s) to complete each sentence.

1 .... are you having for lunch?
   - A When
   - B How
   - C What
   - D Why

2 I'm looking forward .... you.
   - A to meet
   - B for meeting
   - C meet
   - D to meeting

3 Our apartment is .... cosy.
   - A quite
   - B only
   - C quiet
   - D ever

4 Ly can .... a pen from Huang.
   - A lend
   - B borrow
   - C give
   - D offer

5 We .... get up early yesterday.
   - A must
   - B have to
   - C had to
   - D mustn't

6 .... is important in many cultures.
   - A Punctually
   - B Punctual
   - C Be punctual
   - D Punctuality

4 Writing

Write a sentence based on a picture In this part of the test you will write ONE sentence based on a picture. You must use the two words or phrases that are given with the picture.

Example: meetings / break
Possible answer: *We always take a break during meetings.*

1 children / board

2 so / people

Products and services

Unit 3

1 Business situation
Describing products

A 🔊 10 Lisa Yang works for an electronics company in Taipei. She is at a trade show and is answering questions about one of her company's products. Listen and check (✔) the features you hear.

- [ ] alarm clock
- [ ] audio translation
- [ ] backlighting
- [ ] calendar
- [ ] currency converter
- [ ] games
- [ ] LCD screen
- [ ] travel guide
- [ ] USB port
- [ ] voice recorder

B Are the statements true or false? Correct the false statements.

		True	False
1	The man heard about the Lingua Traveler on the radio.	☐	☐
2	Electronic translators have advantages smartphones don't have.	☐	☐
3	The man doesn't like electronic translators.	☐	☐
4	The Lingua Traveler can help you learn a foreign language.	☐	☐
5	All Lingua Traveler models translate eight languages.	☐	☐
6	You can use the Lingua Traveler in the dark.	☐	☐
7	It doesn't matter if you make a spelling mistake.	☐	☐
8	The 03 model costs over $200.	☐	☐

C Work with a partner. Choose a device (for example, your phone or computer) and tell your partner what features it has.

▶ • trade show • feature • native speaker
• to depend (on) • to guess

I can understand someone describing a product.

2 Grammar focus
Focus 1: Review of past simple

A Look at these sentences from the conversation in 1A and complete the chart.

Where **did** you **hear** about it?
They **talked** about it on TV last night.
I **didn't like** the voice quality on my old translator.
I **had** one a few years ago.
It **was** quite simple but very useful.

Simple Past	Statement	Negative	Question
Regular Verbs			
verb 1	they talked	they didn't talk	did they talk?
verb 2			
Irregular Verbs			
verb 1			did you hear?
verb 2			
verb 3		it wasn't	

When a verb ends . . .
– in a vowel and a consonant, we often double the consonant: *stop – stopped*, *plan – planned*.
– in *y*, it changes to *i*: *study – studied*, *try – tried*.

B Complete the text. Use the past simple of the verbs in brackets ( ).

Last week I **1** .... (buy) an electronic translator. I **2** .... (not want) one that **3** .... (be) too expensive. The salesperson **4** .... (advise) me to buy a Lingua Traveler, the simple 01 model. It **5** .... (cost) $150. The last translator I **6** .... (have) **7** .... (not be) very good. It **8** .... (not have) a lot of the features that modern devices have, but when I **9** .... (get) it, it **10** .... (be) the best on the market at that time. But I think the salesperson **11** .... (give) me good advice about the Lingua Traveler. I **12** .... (try) out the new translator as soon as I **13** .... (arrive) home, and it's great.

C Last year Lisa went on a training course. Ask her about it.

1 **You:** Where *did you go*?
   Lisa: To Kaohsiung.
2 **You:** How .... there?
   Lisa: By train.
3 **You:** Where .... ?
   Lisa: In a hotel near Central Park Station.
4 **You:** How long .... ?
   Lisa: Two days.
5 **You:** What .... ?
   Lisa: I learned about my company's new electronic translators.

Kaohsiung

▸ ▪ complicated ▪ device
   ▪ model

I can talk and ask questions using the past simple.

2 Grammar focus
Focus 2: The passive

D 🎧10 Listen to the conversation in 1A again and complete the chart.

Subject	to be	Past particple	
The Lingua Traveler	was	designed	*for* travelers *by* travelers.
Mandarin Chinese	....	....	by over a billion people.
Words and phrases	....	....	on the display.
When the first electronic translators	....	....	the audio quality was poor.

E Complete the rule.

> We form the passive with the verb .... and the past participle of the verb.
>
> We use the passive when:
> - we **know / don't know** who does something:
>   *The bicycle was invented 200 years ago.*
> - it is **important / not important** to say who does something:
>   *Spanish is spoken in many South American countries.*

If we want to say who does something, we use *by*:
Mandarin Chinese is spoken by over a billion people.

F Which sentences are active and which are passive? Write *A* or *P*.

1. **A:** My colleague wrote the reports. ....
   B: The reports were written by my colleague. ....
2. **A:** He left his computer on all night. ....
   B: His computer was left on all night. ....
3. **A:** English is spoken all over the world. ....
   B: Many people all over the world speak English. ....
4. **A:** I made a mistake in my report. ....
   B: My laptop was made in Korea. ....
5. **A:** The offices are cleaned every day. ....
   B: A cleaner cleans our offices every day. ....

G Make sentences in the passive.

1. first computer / build / in 1936   *The first computer was built in 1936.*
2. first smartphones / introduce / in 2007
3. in the 1990s / tapes and CDs / replace / MP3s
4. most expensive cell phone in the world / make / of gold and diamonds
5. about 120 million cell phones / throw away / every year in the US
6. first text message / send / by a Canadian engineer / in 1989
7. about 60,000 videos / post / on YouTube / every week
8. ebay / invent / by a French scientist / in 1995
9. trillions of text messages / send / worldwide / every year
10. Amazon / start / in 1994 / by Jeff Besoz

The most expensive cell phone in the world

▸ display

I can understand and use the passive.

3 Listening and speaking
Describing services

A 🔊 11 Nick Ramos from the Philippines and Akamu Sayavong from Laos are at a conference. Listen to their lunch-break conversation and answer the questions.

1. What is the full name of MLTS?
2. What are the services that MLTS offers?
3. What problems can a Filipino have when he works in Japan?
4. Name three things that you can learn about in cross-cultural training.
5. What is the minimum length of a cross-cultural training course?
6. Who are the trainers in MLTS?
7. What is Nick's job?
8. How is Nick's company doing?

B 🔊 11 Listen again. Which words and phrases does Akamu use to show that he is interested?

- ☐ Can you give me an example?
- ☐ It sounds interesting.
- ☐ Wow! That's amazing.
- ☐ Oh, I see.
- ☐ That's great!
- ☐ Really?
- ☐ That's OK.
- ☐ Right.

C Talking about ... how to learn a foreign language

Step 1: You want to learn a new language. Look at these methods for learning a language and rank them 1 to 6 (1 = the method you like best).

- ☐ private teacher
- ☐ small class with teacher
- ☐ a language app on your phone
- ☐ online self-study
- ☐ online with a teacher
- ☐ a one-month stay in the country

Step 2: Work with a partner. Explain your ranking.

> I ranked a one-month stay in the country as number one because . . .
> A language app on my phone has the lowest ranking because . . .

Your partner uses the phrases from 3B to show that he or she is interested.

Step 3: With a partner, think of the advantages and disadvantages of each method.

Step 4: Find out which method is the most popular in the class. Share your ideas about the advantages and disadvantages of each method.

▷ ▪ belief ▪ custom ▪ ranking

I can understand a conversation about products and services.

22 | Unit 3

4 Vocabulary focus

Focus 1: Adjectives to describe products and services

A These adjectives are from 1A. Can you find four pairs of opposites?

| amazing | difficult | ~~enormous~~ | excellent | interesting | modern |
| new | old | old-fashioned | poor (quality) | simple | ~~tiny~~ |

B Check the meaning of these word pairs in a dictionary and complete the sentences with one of the words.

amazing – amazed   boring – bored   exciting – excited
interesting – interested   disappointing – disappointed   surprising – surprised

Don't mix up *-ed* and *-ing*:

I am interested in your courses. (A person is interested.)

Your course is very interesting. (A thing is interesting.)

1. I'm looking forward to my new job. I'm really e.................
2. Our English lessons are usually i................., but the lesson yesterday was b.................
3. I'm d................. that you didn't buy our product.
4. We didn't enjoy the language course. It was d.................
5. We had an a................. offer from our cell phone provider.
6. Our vacation was organized by a travel agent, and it was really e.................
7. I was s................. that you were so b................. by his presentation.
8. The price was s................. . I was a................. that it was so low.

C Work with a partner.

Student A: Go to Partner file 2.
Student B: Look at the pictures below. Take turns to ask and answer questions about the products. Your partner has to guess what your products are.

A: What is it made of?	B: It's made of plastic / glass / metal / paper.
A: Where do you normally use it?	B: I use it in the kitchen / classroom / office.
A: Which adjectives from 1A and 1B would you use to describe it?	B: It's something modern but very simple.
A: What do you use it for?	B: I use it to . . .

a marker

a bicycle

an English book

a washing machine

a pair of glasses

a printer

I can use different adjectives to describe products and services.

4 Vocabulary focus

Focus 2: ASEAN: countries, languages, and people

D 🎧 12 Listen to a talk about ASEAN. When did the countries join? Put the missing dates on the map.

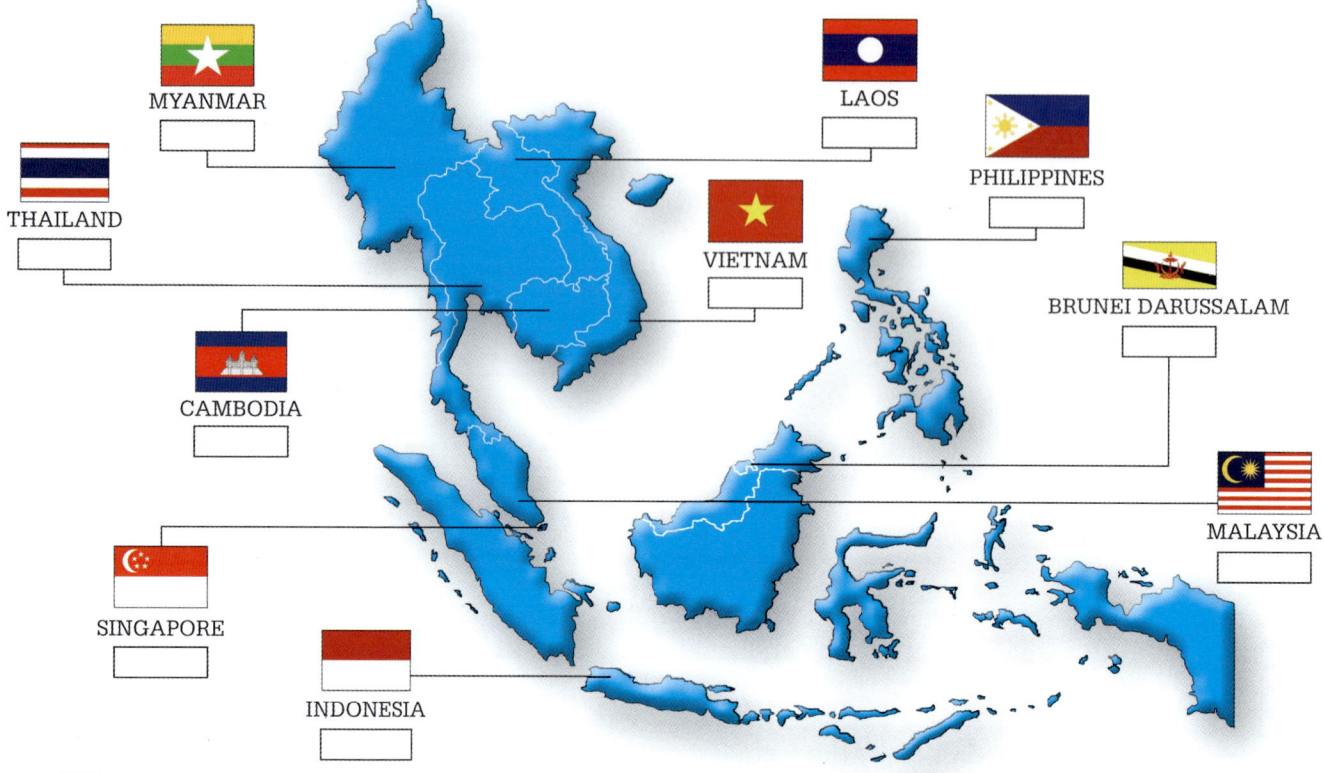

E 🎧 12 Listen again and complete the chart.

Country	Main language(s)	People
Cambodia	Khmer	....
Indonesia	....	Indonesians
Malaysia	Malay, English, ..., Tamil	....
The Philippines	Filipino (Tagalog), English, ...	....
Singapore	English, ..., Chinese, Tamil	Singaporeans
Thailand	Thai	....
Vietnam	....	Vietnamese

F ▷ **Key words** Look at the words at the bottom of pages 19–22. Choose the best word to complete the sentences.

1. The words are shown on the .... or spoken out loud.
2. The Lingua Traveler has lots of special ....
3. You must respect the .... and .... of other cultures.
4. You'll never .... how much I paid for this phone.
5. The store sells all kinds of electronic ....
6. There are about 360 million .... of English in the world.
7. I can't understand your explanation. It's too ....
8. Lisa Yang worked at a .... in Taipei.

I can understand the names of ASEAN countries, languages, and people.

5 Reading
Wearable technology

A) Before you read Which electronic devices do you wear or carry with you every day?

Asian Business **Online**
looks at wearable technologies.

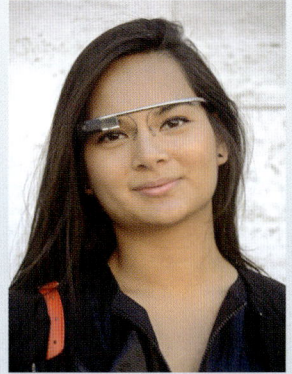

Already millions of people are wearing electronic devices for medical reasons, but the next generation of wearable technologies is just around the corner.

Your day begins when the vibrating alarm clock on your leg wakes you at the best moment for your body. You get quietly out of bed without waking your partner. You put on your high-tech clothes, which will measure how much sunlight there is and automatically protect your skin.

Then you put on your smart glasses. With them you can do everything you can do on a normal computer as you move around. A camera, display, touchpad, battery, and microphone are built into the frames of these glasses, which weigh only 50 grams.

Next you put your smart watch onto your wrist so that you can make calls, display messages, record videos, and take photos while your big phone stays in your pocket.

You decide to bicycle to work. You put on your helmet, which has a special device on top. If you fall and hit your head, the device will send a signal to your smartphone, which is programmed to send for medical help.

After a hard day's work, you arrive home and quickly clean the house with your vacuum shoes that pick up dust while you walk through your home. To relax, just put on your 3D virtual reality headset and you will feel as if you are actually inside a video game. Or you may decide to go jogging and wear your new training shirt. The shirt checks your performance and sends the results to your smartphone.

Yes, these devices already exist, and wearable technology will change our lives. It's just that nobody quite knows how!

B) Skim the text Find:
1. two sentences that talk about clothing.
2. one sentence that talks about road safety.
3. two leisure time activities.

C) Scanning for detail Find which device(s) you wear on . . .
1. your face.
2. your leg.
3. your wrist.
4. your feet.
5. your head.

And which device(s) you wear . . .
6. at night.
7. during the day.
8. on your way to work.
9. after work.

D) Now you Work with a partner. Tell your partner which device interests you most.

I think a . . . is most useful because . . .

I can understand a text about wearable technology.

6 Culture focus
Stereotypes

ster•e•o•type

noun [C] UK 🔊 US 🔊 /ˈsteriətaɪp/

a fixed idea or picture that many people have of a person or thing. Often it is not true in reality.

A In your opinion, which nationalities do these adjectives describe?

formal	....	poor	....
friendly	....	punctual	....
fun-loving	....	quiet	....
hard-working	....	romantic	....
noisy	....	serious	....
rich	....	sporty	....
polite	....		

B Work with a partner. Compare your ideas in 6A. Tell your partner the reasons for your choice.

C 🔊 13 Listen to three people talking about stereotypes and complete the chart.

What do foreigners think about your country?	Jack, Australia	Kavitha, India	Huang, China
The people	....	....	....
Activities	surfing, . . .	....	....
Clothes	....	sari	gray suits
Food	....	....	....

D Work with a partner. What do you think people from other countries think about your country and its people? Make some notes and then tell the class.

People often think that . . .
In fact, that's not true. We . . .

I can discuss stereotypes.

Targeting the customer

Unit 4

1 Business situation
Advertising

A [14] Kang Mi-song from South Korea is working in her company's office in Perth, Australia. She's talking to her colleague Jack Robbins about advertising. Listen to their conversation. Which ways of advertising do they talk about? Check (✔) those you hear.

- [ ] billboards
- [ ] print advertising
- [ ] telemarketing
- [ ] webvertising
- [ ] leaflets
- [ ] social networks
- [ ] TV commercial
- [ ] YouTube

B [14] Listen again and complete the sentences.

1 Mi-song and Jack both saw the .... for Chunky Choc Cookies and liked the .... They both think the .... for hamburgers was funny. They agree that it's silly when a(n) .... promotes something, and they don't believe that a(n) .... is better because somebody .... says they use it.

2 Jack thinks .... is often fun. He likes .... because they make cities more .... He likes to get quick .... about products.

3 Mi-song thinks companies spend too much .... on advertising. She finds .... annoying, and she hates it when advertisers .... her through her phone, but she says she can't live .... it.

C Work in small groups. Think of other ways of advertising that are not in 1A. Which group can find the most ways in five minutes?

▷ ▪ commercial ▪ to go viral ▪ to target
▪ to promote ▪ campaign

I can understand a conversation about advertising.

2 Grammar focus
Focus 1: First conditional

A Look at the sentences about the future.

Jack: I'm sure I'll remember it.
Mi-song: You won't forget the slogan, but will you buy the product?

Complete the rule.

> *I'll* is the short form of *I* ....
> The negative form is *I* ....

"If you really want that promotion, Barnes, you'll swim back to the boat and get my laptop."

B 🔊10 Listen to the conversation in 1A again and complete the sentences in the first conditional.

Jack: If I .... it, I won't buy it.
Mi-song: If we .... their product, we'll be happy.
Jack: If I use the same makeup as a movie star, I .... like her!
Mi-song: If you throw away your phone, the advertisers .... you!

C Underline the correct words to complete the rule.

> First conditional sentences describe "real" situations – things that can or might happen. They have two parts, the condition (*if . . .*) and the result (= *what will happen*).
> For the condition we use *if* + **present simple / future**.
> For the result we use **present simple / future**.

There is no *will* after *if*: If I ~~will~~ like it, I will buy it.

D Complete the sentences. Use the correct form of the verb.

1. If Jack .... (not need) the product, he .... (not buy) it.
2. If Mi-song .... (get) Internet ads, she .... (delete) them.
3. If you .... (like) advertising, you .... (enjoy) the new TV commercials.
4. A company .... (not get) any new customers if it .... (not advertise).
5. If they .... (advertise) on social networking sites, they .... (reach) a lot of people.
6. You .... (not have) much fun if you .... (take) things too seriously.

E Work with a partner. Take turns to ask and answer these questions. Begin your questions with *What will you do if . . . .* Think of two more questions.

1. weather / nice / weekend?
2. go / shopping mall / Saturday?
3. meet / friend / this evening?
4. stay / home / evening?

- slogan - to advertise
- to annoy - to delete

I can understand and use the first conditional.

2 Grammar focus
Focus 2: Adverbs of manner

F Look at these sentences from the conversation in 1A, then read the rule. Are the words in bold adjectives or adverbs?

Don't take things so **seriously**.
Companies can target consumers **quickly** and **cheaply**.
Webvertising is an **easy** way to get new customers.
You can delete the ads **easily**.
I can get **quick** information about products that interest me.

Complete the rule.

> Adjectives describe nouns (people or things).
> Adverbs of manner tells us about a verb: *how* we do things.
> To make an adverb of manner we add .... to an adjective.

These are different:

good → well   fast → fast   hard → hard

He's a good speaker. → He speaks well.
She's a fast driver. → She drives fast.
They are hard workers. → They work hard.

G Underline the correct word.

1 I always cross the road **carefully** / **careful**.
2 I always walk very **fast** / **fastly**.
3 I'm a **good** / **well** listener.
4 I'm a **quiet** / **quietly** person.
5 I eat **slowly** / **slow** and enjoy **good** / **well** food.
6 I'm a very **serious** / **seriously** person.
7 I always study **hard** / **hardly**.
8 I always wait in line **patiently** / **patient**.

I sometimes honk my horn loudly.

H Work with a partner. Read aloud the sentences in 2G that are true for you. Your partner agrees or disagrees.

A: I always cross the road . . .
B: Me, too / Oh, I don't.
A: I don't always . . .
B: Oh, I do / Me, neither.

I Put the words in the correct order.

1 well / speaks / Mi-song / English
2 close / please / quietly / door / the
3 the / report / wrote / quickly / Jack
4 correctly / I / your / did / message / understand ?
5 its / company / pays / badly / the / employees

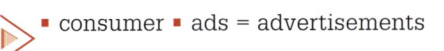

- consumer - ads = advertisements

I can use adverbs of manner to talk about how we do things.

3 Listening and speaking
Radio commercials

A 🔊15 Listen to three radio commercials and complete the chart.

	Name of the product or company	What is the product or service?	What does it promise to do?
1	....	....	....
2	Up and Away	....	....
3	....	....	....

B Work with a partner. Think about a TV or radio commercial that you like. Tell a partner your ideas.

I think the commercial for . . . is original / funny / catchy / romantic / silly because . . .

C Talking about . . . advertising

Step 1: Think about these situations.

1. You want to sell a new computer program that helps students pass their exams. How will you advertise it?

2. You need somebody to share your apartment. Decide how to advertise it so you can find the type of person you want to live with.

3. You have a small local coffee shop. You don't have much money, so you need to think carefully about how and where to advertise.

4. Your company makes plastic bottles for soft drinks. You want new customers. Decide who the customers are and how to attract them.

Step 2: Work in a small group and share your ideas.

I think the best place/way to advertise a new program for students is . . . because . . .

Step 3: Present your ideas to the class and discuss them.

▷ ▪ to solve ▪ technician
  ▪ satisfied ▪ to damage

I can understand commercials and talk about advertising.

Unit 4

4 Vocabulary focus
Focus 1: Advertising words

A Match words 1 to 10 with definitions A to J.

1	commercial	E	A	a famous person
2	consumer	....	B	a phrase that is easy to remember
3	billboard	....	C	advertising on the Internet
4	celebrity	....	D	ads in newspapers and magazines
5	slogan	....	E	advertisement on TV or radio
6	print advertising	....	F	short form of "advertisement"
7	webvertising	....	G	spread quickly
8	go viral	....	H	a piece of paper with information
9	leaflet	....	I	advertising in the street
10	ad	....	J	a person who buys and uses things

B Which words go together? Check (✔) two words for numbers 1 to 7.

1	advertising	✔	campaign	✔	slogan	☐	product
2	catchy	☐	tune	☐	company	☐	slogan
3	target	☐	billboards	☐	customers	☐	consumers
4	delete	☐	an ad	☐	a message	☐	a product
5	colorful	☐	ad	☐	service	☐	billboard
6	sales	☐	slogan	☐	department	☐	conference
7	promote	☐	a product	☐	an event	☐	prices

C Complete the text with words from 4A and 4B.

Rio Okazaki and Hiroto Okada started their soft drinks **1** c................. last year. They were sure they had a great **2** p..................., but then they had to decide how to **3** p................ it and how to **4** t.................. their future **5** c................... At first, they talked about a TV **6** c.................. with a catchy **7** s..................., but that was too expensive. They thought about handing out **8** l.................. on the street, but they decided they couldn't reach enough people. Then they discussed **9** p.................. a.................. – some **10** c.................. ads in magazines and **11** n................... Finally, they decided that **12** w.................. on the Internet was probably the cheapest way to advertise, and with a bit of luck their **13** a.................. would go **14** v...................

D What is the advertising word?

1	gliteneemkart	t...................
2	nitrp nisdertigav	p.................. a..................
3	arretvedis	a...................
4	feetall	l...................
5	dortpuc	p...................
6	naglos	s...................
7	lascio westnrok	s................... n...................

I can understand and use advertising words.

4 Vocabulary focus
Focus 2: Easily confused words (1)

E Complete the sentences with *if* or *when*.

if = it may happen   *when* = it is sure to happen

1 .... I'm sick tomorrow, I won't go to work.
2 .... the meeting finishes, we'll go for lunch.
3 .... the plane lands, I'll call you.
4 .... you are out when I call, I'll leave a message.
5 I'll be surprised .... you don't get the job.
6 I'll have to work late tonight .... my boss asks me to.
7 .... you wake up tomorrow, I'll be in New York.

When she buys those shoes, she will get a pair free.

F 🎧16 Listen to the sentences. Put a ✔ when you hear *quiet* and ✘ when you hear *quite*.

quiet = opposite of *noisy*   *quite* = not a lot, but not a little

1	2	3	4	5	6
✔	✘				

G Put the words in the correct order. Add *to* if necessary.

1 tells / that / advertising / Mi-song / he / likes / Jack
2 say / she / what / Jack / did ?
3 the / you / tell / can / time / me ?
4 teacher / something / I / my / said
5 told / funny / a / boss / us / our / joke

> *Tell* is followed by a person:
> Can you <u>tell me</u> the way to the station?
>
> *Say* is not followed by a person: What did he <u>say</u>?
>
> BUT *say* + *to* + person:
> What did he <u>say to</u> you?

H ▶ **Key words** Look at the words at the bottom of pages 27–30. Choose the best words to complete the sentences.

1 Our .... can help you to .... your problems.
2 A lot of companies .... children with their TV ....
3 We hope that our customers are .... with our service.
4 Every company hopes its Internet ads will ....
5 The advertising .... was a great success.
6 Sorry, I .... your email. Can you send it again?
7 I don't like Internet ads. It .... me.
8 Too much sun can .... your hair.

I can use some easily confused words correctly.

5 Reading
An advertising trend

A) Before you read Look at the pictures. Describe what you see. What do you think the article will be about?

Asian Business **Online**
looks at "insight selling."

Tom Tsai lives in Taiwan and he loves bicycling. The Taiwanese capital, Taipei, has a large number of bike shops, and Tom knows that his store, Bike Paradise, needs to offer customers more than fair prices and good service. "Most people who come here already have a lot of information from the Internet about our products," he says, "so we have to offer something else – we have to sell them a lifestyle, an experience."

Advertisers call this "insight selling" – not just giving consumers the hard sell, but learning about the customer in order to offer a product in a new way. "For example, I bicycle through the city every day, and it's important for me to find safe routes. I use digital media to share this information with my customers. We also organize bike rides and give lessons in bike maintenance. People want to be part of something, and they'll come to us because we take care of them."

Andy Chen also uses insight selling to market his chain of health food stores, Veggies-and-More. He takes time to learn about his customers and understand their lifestyles. Andy opened his first store in 2008 and now has three on the island.

While his products are still the same, his advertising strategy has changed. "When we first started, we used print advertising, but that wasn't very successful. So now we spend the money on social media. I can reach customers directly and send them product information and health and diet tips linked to products they can buy in the store."

Not only small businesses but also multinational companies use insight selling. Volkswagen, for example, discovered that buyers of the new Golf GTI were young men who liked playing games on their phones. So VW offered an app for a GTI game. Downloads reached over four million – a small investment with a huge impact!

B) The main idea Which sentence give the main idea of the text? A, B, or C?

A Knowing the customer is more important than pushing the product.
B Traditional forms of advertising are not effective.
C There are many successful small businesses in Taiwan.

C) Scanning for detail Are the statements correct? If not, correct them.

1 Most of Tom Tsai's customers come to the shop for information about the products.
2 Tom Tsai goes to work by bike.
3 Bike Paradise offers customers more than just a product.
4 Veggies-and-More has different products today than in 2008.
5 For his first shop Andy advertised in magazines and newspapers.
6 VW's advertising campaign for the Golf GTI was inexpensive and effective.

D) Vocabulary Find words in the text to complete these sentences.

1 At Bike Paradise, the prices are .... and the .... is good.
2 "Insight selling" means not just giving customers the ....
3 Tom Tsai tells his customers about .... for bicycling through the city.
4 At Veggies-and-More you can buy ....
5 Andy uses .... to reach his customers directly.

I can understand a text about an advertising trend.

6 Business writing
Formal and informal language in emails

A Hattie Smith is back in her London office after a business trip to Tokyo. She is writing two emails.

1. Which email is to a colleague?
2. Which email is to a friend?
3. What's the difference?

1

To: Richard Miles <rmiles@tecwol.com>
From: Hattie Smith <hsmith@tecwol.com>
Subject: Tokyo trip
Cc: Karen Lee <klee@tecwol.com>
Attachments: Reports

Dear Richard:

Just to let you know that I am back in the office after the Tokyo trip. I am rather tired after the long flight, but the trip was very productive. I was warmly welcomed. I met with the design team and the head of the marketing department. Please find attached reports of those meetings.

Shota Yamamoto had some questions about the Asia conference that I couldn't answer. I am sure Karen can be of assistance. I am copying her so that she can contact him.

I will give you more details of the trip at the meeting tomorrow.

Best regards,
Hattie

2

To: Kathy Gordon <kgordon1@icloud.com>
From: Hattie Smith <hsmith@tecwol.com>
Subject: I'm back!
Cc:
Attachments: pics

Hi Kath,

Well, I'm back in the office – and feeling pretty dead after the long flight from Tokyo. But it was a great trip and the people were so nice. I felt really welcome there.

I had a bit of time for sightseeing and I loved the city. ☺ I attach a couple of pics. It was a pity it rained so much that day. ☹ And guess what – there was an earthquake!!! Well, just a little one. Nobody was worried except me. They're used to them!

Please give me a call asap so I can tell you more.

Best,
Hattie

B Write *F* if the statement is about a formal email and *I* if it's about an informal email. Find examples in the emails.

1. Use a lot of short forms like *don't, we're, hasn't,* etc. ... I
2. Use abbreviations like *asap, 2nite.* ....
3. Passive forms are often used: *The goods were delivered yesterday.* ....
4. Formal words such as *assistance, productive, request,* and *rather* are used. ....
5. Use emoticons and smileys: ☺ ☹. ....
6. Informal words such as *fantastic, great, a bit of* are used. ....
7. Exclamation marks (!) show surprise or other strong feelings. ....

C Look at Karen Lee's email to Shota Yamamoto. Rewrite it in a more formal way.

Hello Mr. Yamamoto,

Hattie Smith told me that you asked for some information about the Asia conference. I'm a little busy, so here's our sales report, and I'll give you a call asap.

Bye,
Karen Lee

I can recognize formal and informal language.

TOEIC® practice

1 Listening

A 🔊 17 Conversations Listen and answer the questions.

Conversation 1

1. The woman talks about a commercial. For which product?
   - [ ] A a sports store
   - [ ] B a TV
   - [ ] C a car
   - [ ] D a skateboard

2. Which statement is correct?
   - [ ] A The man watched TV yesterday.
   - [ ] B The woman watched TV yesterday.
   - [ ] C The woman didn't like the commercial she saw.
   - [ ] D The man and the woman saw the same commercial.

3. What does the man say about commercials?
   - [ ] A He has some favorites.
   - [ ] B He never watches them.
   - [ ] C He doesn't like them.
   - [ ] D He thinks some of them are good.

Conversation 2

1. When will the speakers meet?
   - [ ] A 10 AM
   - [ ] B 11 AM
   - [ ] C 12 AM
   - [ ] D 1 PM

2. Where will the speakers meet?
   - [ ] A at the meeting
   - [ ] B over lunch
   - [ ] C in the man's office
   - [ ] D in the woman's office

3. What will the woman bring with her?
   - [ ] A a sales report
   - [ ] B a news report
   - [ ] C coffee
   - [ ] D lunch

B 🔊 18 Question-Response Listen carefully. Choose the best response to the sentence you hear.

Example: What did the customer buy?
A [ ] By tomorrow.   B [✓] A thumb drive.   C [ ] He didn't buy it.

1 A [ ] B [ ] C [ ]   3 A [ ] B [ ] C [ ]
2 A [ ] B [ ] C [ ]   4 A [ ] B [ ] C [ ]

2 Speaking

Describe a picture Look at the picture for 30 seconds, then describe it in your own words.

3 Reading

Text completion Read the passage. Choose the best word to complete each sentence.

College starts again next week after the summer vacation, and producers of electronic translators hope to increase **1** .... this autumn.

- [ ] A repairs
- [ ] B sales
- [ ] C customers
- [ ] D prices

A widespread advertising **2** .... began last week

- [ ] A report
- [ ] B commercial
- [ ] C campaign
- [ ] D product

3 .... TV, the radio, and the Internet.

- [ ] A in
- [ ] B by
- [ ] C at
- [ ] D on

Companies are also targeting students directly with ads in teenage magazines **4** .... *Teen Life* and *Glitter*.

- [ ] A as
- [ ] B such as
- [ ] C example
- [ ] D examples

4 Writing

Respond to a written request Reply to the email. Ask for at least TWO more pieces of information.

> From: Tecwol Marketing Department
> To: Tecwol heads of department
> Subject: Reservations for annual conference
>
> ---
>
> Our annual conference will take place in the Premier Hotel at 34 Park Road on June 3 at 2 PM. We need to make reservations for the rooms and dinner. Please let us know by the end of the week how many rooms your department will need. Could you also let us know if the participants will attend the evening dinner and if anyone requires vegetarian or other special meals?

Unit 5

Achievements

1 Business situation
Presenting facts and figures

A 🔊 19 Yi Ling Tan works for an electronics company in Singapore. She is giving a presentation about her company's sales figures to a new group of trainees. Listen to her presentation and decide if she is talking about Table 1 or Table 2.

Table 1

Exports in millions of US dollars			
	Year before last	Last year	This year
Asia	48	50	52
Europe	30	32	33
North America	26	27	29
South America	–	–	20
Total	104	109	134

Table 2

Exports in millions of US dollars			
	Year before last	Last year	This year
Asia	48	50	52
Europe	30	32	28
North America	28	27	29
South America	–	–	–
Total	106	109	109

B Look at your answer to 1A and choose the correct word.

1 Last year, exports to Asia **increased / decreased** compared with the year before.
2 This year, exports to Asia **have risen / have fallen** again.
3 Last year, exports to Europe **fell / rose** compared with the year before.
4 This year, exports to Europe **have fallen / have risen**.
5 Total exports this year **have risen / have fallen / have stayed the same** compared with last year.

increase = rise (– rose – risen)
decrease = fall (– fell – fallen)

▷ • achievement • figures • to increase
• to rise • to decrease

I can understand a presentation of sales figures.

2 Grammar focus
Focus 1: Present perfect

A 🔊19 Listen to the presentation again and complete the sentences.

1 Last year, the company .... products worth US$50 million to Asia.
2 We .... goods worth US$52 million to Asia so far.
3 Last year, exports to Europe .... compared with the year before.
4 This year, they ....
5 Last year, exports to North America .... to US$27 million.
6 This year, exports there ....
7 Two years ago, we .... up new markets in North America.
8 This year, we .... up new markets in South America.

B Underline the time phrases in the sentences in 2A and put them in the correct box. There are two phrases for each box.

Time in the past (= time is "finished")	Time from the past to the present (= time is "not finished")
last year	....
....	....

What's the rule? Underline the correct tense.

> We form the present perfect with *have* + the past participle of the verb.
>
> When we talk about time that is "not finished," we use the **past simple / present perfect**.
>
> When we talk about time that is "finished," we use the **past simple / present perfect**.

> The past participle of regular verbs is the same as the past simple:
>
> export – exported – <u>exported</u>   increase – increased – <u>increased</u>
>
> For irregular verbs, see the list on pages 95.

C Work with a partner. Ask each other two questions. Use the simple past and the present perfect.

1 write an email **today** / **yesterday**
   A: *Have you written an email today?*
   B: *Yes, I have. / No, I haven't.*
   A: *Did you write an email yesterday?*
   B: *Yes, I did. / No, I didn't.*
2 send a lot of text messages **this week** / **last week**
3 give a presentation in class **this semester** / **last semester**
4 play a computer game **today** / **yesterday**
5 take a vacation **this year** / **last year**

2 Grammar focus
Focus 2: *Since* and *for*

D Read about Yi Ling Tan. With a partner, complete the questions and answer them.

Yi Ling Tang works for an electronics company in Singapore. She's worked there since February last year. Before that, she worked for three years for an airline company. She's lived in Singapore since she got married. She and her husband live in an apartment in eastern Singapore. They've lived there for only a few months. They lived in a downtown apartment for two years, but it was very expensive. Yi Ling's husband is a chef. He worked at the Shangri-La Hotel for a long time. Since September, he's had his own restaurant.

1 How long *has* Yi Ling Tang *worked* for the electronics company?
   She's worked for the electronics company since February last year.
2 How long *did* she *work* for the airline company?
   She worked for the airline company for three years.
3 How long .... she .... in Singapore?
4 How long .... they .... in eastern Singapore?
5 How long .... they .... downtown?
6 How long .... Yi Ling Tang's husband .... at the Shangri-La Hotel?
7 How long .... he .... his own restaurant?

E Write all the words and phrases with *since* and *for* in 2D.

since: *February,* ....
for: *three years,* ....

What's the rule? Underline the correct word.

> We use *for* with a **period** / **point** of time.
> We use *since* with a **period** / **point** of time in the past.

F Work with a partner.
Student A: Look at Partner file 3.
Student B: Look at your profile.
Answer your partner's questions.

He's a chef = He is . . .
He's been to China. = He has . . .

I'm a web designer. I work in Sydney, Australia, for an advertising company. I started to work there two years ago. Before that, I worked for a hotel chain. That was in Sydney, too. I worked there for three years. I live in Sydney in a downtown apartment. I moved there one year ago. I lived in the suburbs for a long time, but I got fed up with commuting to work. And the apartment was old. My new apartment is smaller, but it's modern.

Now ask your partner these questions.

What do you do?	Where do you live?
Where do you work?	How long have you lived there?
How long have you worked there?	What kind of apartment do you live in?
Where did you work before?	What kind of apartment did you live in before?
How long did you work there?	Why did you move?

▸ ▪ downtown ▪ chef
  ▪ profile ▪ chain

I can use the present perfect with *for* and *since*.

3 Listening and speaking
Personal achievements

A 🔊 20 Listen to the radio interview with sports store owner Sebastian Patel. In the text below there are 12 mistakes. Listen and correct the mistakes.

Sebastian Patel was born in London in 1976. His father came from India and his mother was Indian, too. They lived in a wealthy district of London. In his free time, Sebastian ran with his mother through the city's parks.

Sebastian ran his first race at school. Nobody was surprised how fast he could run. His father coached him, and when he was only eighteen, he ran 800 metres in one minute fifteen seconds.

In the last five years, he has opened two successful sports stores. This year, Sebastian Patel has given a million pounds to build a sports stadium in the London district where he lives. He wants poor kids there to have a chance to watch sports because sports may be the way to a better future.

B 🔊 20 Listen to the interview again. Complete the sentences.

1. Before he became a successful businessman, Sebastian was ....
2. In 1976, Sebastian's father ....
3. Sebastian went running in his free time because ....
4. Five years ago, Sebastian ....

C Talking about ... successful people

Step 1: In groups of three, agree on a successful person you want to talk about – in business, sports, or entertainment. It can be a real person or somebody you invent.

Step 2: Research the person on the Internet and make notes. (Or invent the details yourself.) Find out about:
- where and when the person was born.
- where and when he/she went to school/college.
- how his/her career began.
- how the person became famous/successful.
- what he/she has achieved in life so far.

Step 3: Share your information in your group and prepare a short group presentation. Decide who in the group will give which information.

Step 4: Tell the class about your person.

... was born ...   ... studied ... at ...   ... trained as a ...
... began his/her career in ...
... has been a ... since/for ...   ... became famous when ...
... has achieved ... so far ...

▷ ▪ wealthy ▪ district
▪ to coach ▪ competition

I can understand and talk about successful people.

40 | Unit 5

4 Vocabulary focus
Focus 1: Graphs and charts

A Name the graphs and charts with words from the box

pie chart   bar chart   line graph

  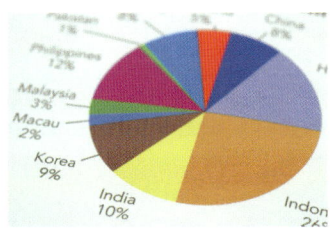

1 .... 2 .... 3 ....

B Which charts A to C and words 1 to 9 describe the graphs?

  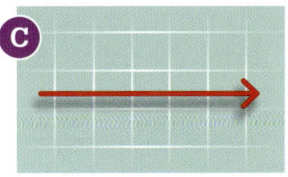

1 drop   A
2 increase   ....
3 stay the same   ....
4 fall   ....
5 rise   ....
6 go up   ....
7 go down   ....
8 climb   ....
9 decrease   ....

> *The sun rises in the east. (rise – rose – risen)*
> *You raise your hand to ask a question. (raise – raised – raised)*

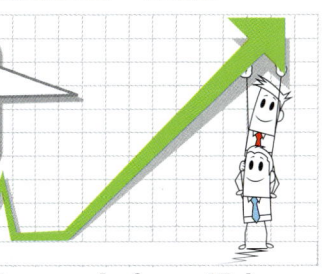

C Look at the bar chart. Complete the sentences with one of the words from 4B in the correct form. Use each word only once.

1 Bangkok Bikes sold 300 bikes in January. In February, sales .... to 200.
2 In March, sales ...., but in April, they ....
3 In May, sales .... to 500 and continued to .... until August, which was the best month of the year.
4 In September, sales began to .... Sales .... in October, but .... again in November.
5 In December, as a result of Christmas sales, the figures .... again.

I can describe graphs and charts.

Unit 5

4 Vocabulary focus
Focus 2: Presenting information

D 🔊 21 Listen to Peter Garcia describing his company. Complete the text.

Good morning. My name is Peter Garcia. Today, I'd like to tell you something about my ...., Solar Light. It was .... in 2010 and is .... in Manila. Solar Light .... high-quality solar panels. Our main .... are solar energy companies in Asia. Solar Light has 45 .... in the office, the ...., and in sales. We have .... of US$5 million per year. That's all I want to tell you today. If you have any questions, please ask me.

E 🔊 21 Listen to Peter Garcia's presentation again. How does he:

- open his presentation?
  Good morning. My ....
- close his presentation?
  That's all ....

Here are some other phrases. Write O (opening) or C (closing).

1 So, I've come to the end of my presentation. Do you have any questions? ....
2 My topic today is . . . .
3 Finally, I'd like to . . . .
4 I'd like to begin by . . . .
5 My presentations will deal with . . . .
6 Thank you for listening. ....

It's simple. Any questions?

F 🔊 19 Listen to the presentation in 1A again. Check (✔) the connecting words you hear.

☐ as a result   ☐ first   ☐ however
☐ because   ☐ finally   ☐ if
☐ but   ☐ for example ☐ so that

G Underline the correct words.

1 Bangkok Bikes had a good month in August. **So that** / **However**, sales were low for the rest of the year.
2 **First,** / **Finally,** I want to finish my presentation with some figures.
3 They had financial problems. **As a result,** / **For example,** they went out of business.
4 Sebastian built a sports club so **that** / **because** poor kids could do sports.
5 **But** / **If** you have any questions, you can ask Peter Garcia.

H ▶ **Key words** Look at the words at the bottom of pages 37–40. Choose the best words to complete the sentences.

1 It will be a great .... if you pass your exams.
2 I have never won a .... in my life.
3 My office isn't ...., it's in the suburbs.
4 The opposite of poor is ....
5 Which .... of Hong Kong do you live in?
6 Unfortunately, sales this year have ....
7 Last year's sales .... were better than this year's.
8 Holiday Inn is an international hotel ....

I can open and close a presentation and use connecting words.

42 | Unit 5

5 Reading
Successful Asian businesspeople

A Before you read Skim the text and find out what sort of businesses the two successful people run.

Asian Business Online
looks at two successful Asian businesspeople.

Yusaku Maezawa didn't want to be a businessman. He was a member of a Japanese punk band and was happy to play his drums. He wanted to share his favorite music with everyone, so in the mid-1990s, he started to sell music CDs and T-shirts online from his kitchen table. In 2004, he had the idea of the online shopping mall and Zozotown, the fashion mall, was born. Since then, sales have increased by 20 percent a year. Today the Zozotown website has over six million members who can shop at 621 stores.

At the age of 35, Yusaku Maezawa was already a billionaire. But he is not only a good businessman, he also has a big heart. After the 2011 earthquake and tsunami, he sold special T-shirts in his online store and raised $3.7 million for the Japanese Red Cross.

Haan Gyung-hee was a homemaker in South Korea with a problem: how to keep the floors clean and not spend hours doing it. Because of the *ondol* tradition of heating homes through the floor, Koreans spend a lot of time on the floor. They sit, sleep, eat, and play on it, so it is very important to keep it clean. Gyung-hee didn't want to be on her hands and knees every day washing the floor, so she invented a steam cleaner.

Many people didn't take Gyung-hee seriously, and it was difficult for her to get a bank loan to go into business. But in 1999, she succeeded. Now Haan Gyung-hee is the CEO of a multinational, multimillion-dollar company called Haan Corporation. Since the first idea for the floor cleaner, Gyung-hee has had many other good ideas for new products, such as a clothes steamer for ironing clothes. As a result, her company is doing very well.

B Scanning for detail What happened in:
1 1999?   2 2004?   3 2011?   4 the mid-1990s?

C Comprehension Complete the sentences.
1 Before he went into business, Yusaku Maezawa was ....
2 He started to sell music CDs because he ....
3 Since 2004, Zozotown sales ....
4 .... to raise money for the Japanese Red Cross.
5 A clean floor is very important in Korea because ....
6 Haan Gyung-hee didn't want to clean floors on her hands and knees, so she ....
7 Haan Corporation is a ....

D Now you You have enough money to start a new business. What business do you want to start? Why?

I've chosen . . . The reason for this is that . . .

I can understand a text about successful Asian businesspeople.

6 Culture focus
Hand signals

A Look at the hand signals that are often used in the US and the UK. Match pictures A to H with the correct expressions 1 to 8.

A   B   C   D

E   F   G   H

1 Just stop right there!	5 Great job! Well done! ....
2 I've no idea.	6 That's a bad idea. ....
3 Hope everything goes well.	7 You must be crazy! ....
4 Call me.	8 Sorry, I can't hear you. ....

B 🎧22 Listen to speakers 1 to 8. Which hand signals from 6A are they giving while they speak?

1 [F]   2 ☐   3 ☐   4 ☐   5 ☐   6 ☐   7 ☐   8 ☐

C Which of the hand signals A to H can you use in these following situations?

1 A colleague asks you for some information, but you can't help. ....
2 You're at a very noisy party and somebody is trying to tell you something. ....
3 A friend of yours is going on a job interview. ....
4 Somebody wants to have an argument with you, but you don't want to argue. ....
5 Your colleague has written an excellent report. ....
6 You want to keep in touch with somebody. ....
7 A friend asks you about a movie you have seen. It was a very bad movie. ....
8 A friend thinks you should invest all your money in his new business. ....

D Do you use these hand signals in your country? Do they have the same meaning? Think of another hand signal that is used in your country. Explain it to your partner. Then change roles.

I can understand typical hand signals.

How would you like to pay?

Unit 6

1 Business situation
Banks and their services

A 🔊 23 Kasem Wattana works for a bank in Bangkok. Listen to the conversations and match the person with the requests.

1 May Watson		A take out a loan.
2 Mr. O'Brian	wants to	B cash checks.
3 The American woman		C open an account.

B 🔊 23 Listen to the conversations again and complete the sentences with words from the box.

| ATM | bank transfer | borrow | checking | exchange |
| lend | loan | salary | savings | sign | traveler's checks |

1 What kind of account would you like? A(n) .... account or a(n) .... account?
2 My employer will deposit my .... into my account.
3 You can pay your bills by .... or get cash from a(n) ....
4 I'd like the bank to give me a(n) ....
5 I can open a second shop if the bank can .... me the money.
6 How much do you want to .... ?
7 I want to change some money. What's the .... rate?
8 Please .... the .... and take them to the desk over there.

▷ ▪ account ▪ salary ▪ to lend
▪ to borrow ▪ loan

I can understand conversations in a bank.

Unit 6 45

2 Grammar focus
Focus 1: Verbs + object + *to do*

A 🔊 23 Listen to the conversations in 1A again and complete the sentences.

1 I **want** my employer .... my salary into a bank account.
2 May I **ask** you .... out this form.
3 I'**d like** the bank .... me a loan.
4 I'll **get** her secretary .... you an appointment.
5 Can you **help** me .... some money?

B Complete the rule.

> *want* / *ask* / *would like* / will *get* / *help* + object + ... + verb

C Report what was said. Use the verbs in brackets ( ).

> We use the same rule for the verbs *advise*, *expect*, and *tell*:
> The bank manager <u>advised me to</u> open a savings account.
> We <u>expected the bank to</u> give us a loan.
> Who <u>told you to</u> invest your money like that?

1 "Please sign the checks," Kasem said to the tourist. (*tell*)
   Kasem told the tourist to sign the checks.
2 "Would you fill out the form, please?" Kasem said to Ms. Watson. (*ask*)
3 "Talk to Ms. Mookjai," Kasem said to the customer. (*advise*)
4 "Can you help me?" the American woman said to Kasem. (*want*)
5 "Please give Mr. O'Brian an appointment," Kasem said to the secretary. (*would like*)

D Look at the pictures. Say what you *will get* the people to do.

1 photographer – take
2 bank manager – give
3 travel agent – book
4 car mechanic – fix
5 delivery person – bring

I'll get the photographer to take my picture.

E Work with a partner. Take turns to talk about yourself.

1 When I was a teenager, my parents always wanted me to ....
2 They advised me to ....
3 I don't want my friends to ....
4 I expect my friends to ....
5 I often get somebody to ....

▷ • photographer • car mechanic
  • delivery person

I can use verbs + object + to do.

2 Grammar focus
Focus 2: Defining relative clauses

F Look at the sentences from 1A and complete the rule.

I've found a job **that** starts next week.
Most people **who** need an account for their salary choose a checking account.
There's a shop **which** is empty.
She's the person **that** deals with the loans.

> Defining relative clauses give us more information about people or things.
> Defining relative clauses about . . .
> – people begin with .... or ....
> – things begin with .... or ....

G Complete the sentences with *who*, *which*, or *that*. Then compare with a partner.

1 The person .... asked Kasem for help was a tourist.
2 The shops .... are in the Riverfront Mall are very popular.
3 Ms. Mookjai was the person .... advised Mr. O'Brian.
4 I'd like a job .... lets me work from home.
5 Customers sometimes ask questions .... are difficult to answer.

With that loan that you give me I'd like to buy the bank.

H Look at these sentences from the conversations in 1A. Complete the sentences with *who*, *which*, or *that*.

> When the relative pronoun is the subject, we use *who*, *which*, or *that*.
> When the relative pronoun is the object, we can leave it out.

1 You remember the business ▲ I started last year? ....
2 Souvenir Land – the shop ▲ you opened in the Riverfront shopping mall. ....
3 She was the lady ▲ I spoke to last time. ....
4 The checks ▲ I have are for 100 dollars each. ....

I Make sentences that are true for you. Tell a partner.

1 I like people who . . .
2 I don't like people who . . .
3 A TV program that makes me laugh is . . .
4 The person who knows me best is . . .
5 The language I speak best is . . .
6 The music I like best is . . .
7 The best teacher is a person who . . .
8 The food I eat most often is . . .
9 I'd like a job which . . .

A TV program that makes me laugh

I can use defining relative clauses.

3 Listening and speaking
A company and its money

A [24] Three years ago, Nuri Susanti and Yandi Susanto started their company, Choc-o-Bars, in Surabaya, Indonesia. Listen to the interview and decide if the statements are true or false. Correct the false statements.

		True	False
1	Nuri heard a news report about chocolate sales in Asia.	☐	☐
2	Nuri and Yandi had enough savings to start their business.	☐	☐
3	The bank manager couldn't help them.	☐	☐
4	They bought all of their equipment secondhand.	☐	☐
5	They can't find good staff to work for them.	☐	☐
6	They look for discounts and hunt for bargains.	☐	☐
7	They only advertise on the Internet.	☐	☐
8	They advise their customers to pay by credit card.	☐	☐
9	Their company has taken a loss for the last two years.	☐	☐
10	They don't want to sell their company.	☐	☐

B Work with a partner.

Student A: Go to Partner file 4.
Student B: Read your roles and do the role plays.

Role play 1	Role play 2
You work in a bank in Jakarta. An Australian customer comes in. <ul><li>Greet the customer. (*Good . . .*)</li><li>Find out what the customer wants. (*How can . . . ?*)</li><li>Help the customer as much as possible yourself. (*Let me see . . .*)</li><li>If necessary, send the customer to a colleague or arrange an appointment. (*You need to talk to . . .*)</li></ul>	**You are an American tourist in Hong Kong.** You want to change some traveler's checks. You are in a bank. Ask about the exchange rate and decide how much you want to change.

▷ ▪ bargain ▪ discount ▪ currency
▪ loss ▪ profit

I can understand an interview about a company and its money.

4 Vocabulary focus
Focus 1: Dealing with money

A 🔊 25 Listen to the conversations. Match each conversation 1 to 4 with pictures A to D.

A ☐   B ☐   C ☐   D ☐

B Complete the sentences with words from the box.

| change | check | debit | expiration | interest | invest | note | receipt |

1 I gave you a £50 .... and you've given me .... for £20.
2 What's the .... date of your card?
3 Here's your .... I hope you enjoyed your meal.
4 Can I pay by .... card?
5 Here's your card and your ....
6 I want to .... some money and I'd like to know where I can get the most ....

> Customers *borrow* money from banks. (borrow – borrowed – borrowed)
> Banks *lend* money to customers. (lend – lent – lent)

C Choose the correct word.

1 We can pay our bills by bank **statement / transfer**.
2 If you have a savings account, you get **interest / discount**.
3 I needed a new car, so I got a **loan / lend** from the bank.
4 The bank will advise you how to invest your **account / savings**.
5 You should never **borrow / lend** money from friends or **borrow / lend** money to friends.
6 I get angry when people **borrow / lend** things and don't give them back.
7 If you are going abroad, you will need foreign **currency / cash**.
8 Choc-o-Bars was very happy when it made a **loss / profit**.

D Match a sentence beginning (1–6) with an ending (A–F) and add a preposition.

1 I paid the bill	by
2 I don't spend much money	....
3 She didn't get much interest	....
4 Be sure to take good care	....
5 I took some cash	....
6 We don't have much money left	....

A your money.
B bank transfer.
C the ATM.
D our account.
E clothes.
F her savings.

My lucky number!!

E Work in small groups and answer the questions.

1 What do these expressions mean?
   A "Money doesn't grow on trees."
   B "Do you think I'm made of money?"
2 If you had no money, could you be happy?

> *I can* use different words to talk about money.

4 Vocabulary focus
Focus 2: Foreign currencies

F |26| Listen to the names for the symbols. Write the currencies below next to the right country flag in the app. Find out the correct rate for $1 and write it in too.

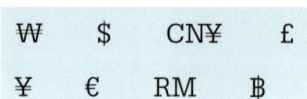

W $ CN¥   £
¥   €   RM   ฿

G |27| Work in pairs. Read these sentences aloud. Then listen and check.

1 The Swiss chocolate company was bought for only ¥65 million.
2 The London-based company made a profit of £13 million last year.
3 The Green Corn Company's revenue for this year stands at US$3.5 million.
4 The average salary for bank tellers in Germany is now €2,520 per month.
5 At ¥ 2,950,234, the new Toyota is a bargain.
6 The average price for a five-star hotel room in Bangkok has risen to ฿5,500 per night.

H |28| Listen and correct these numbers and currencies.

1 US$1,140,136 ....
2 ¥2,122,987 ....
3 €23,465 ....
4 CN¥509,646 ....
5 ฿94,540 ....
6 ₩3,678,233 ....
7 RM99,945 ....
8 £5,123,654 ....

I |29| Listen and fill in the amounts in the checks. Then practice saying the numbers.

1 $ ....
2 ₩ ....
3 € ....
4 ฿ ....
5 ¥ ....
6 RM ....

J Work with a partner. Each write down four long numbers. Dictate your numbers to your partner. Then check what your partner has written.

K ▷ **Key words** Look at the words at the bottom of pages 45–48. Choose the best words to complete the sentences.

1 We got a .... to fix our car.
2 We got our new car at a really good price. It was a ....
3 We got a 20 percent .... on our restaurant meal.
4 My employer deposits my .... into my checking ....
5 The pound sterling is the .... of Great Britain.
6 I need a bank .... to buy an apartment.
7 If a company spends more than it earns, it makes a ....
8 Why don't you get a .... to take some pictures?

I can talk about different currencies.

50 | Unit 6

5 Reading
Group buying

A) Before you read Do you look for bargains when you are shopping? How can you save money?

Asian Business Online
looks at deal-of-the day websites.

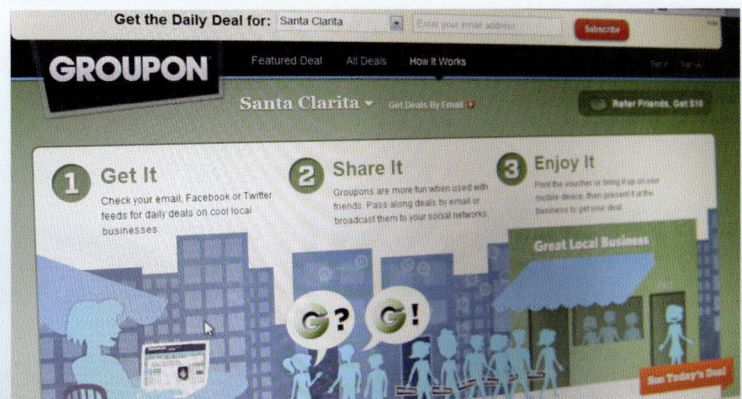

Did you know that the couple at the table next to yours in the restaurant in Shanghai got a 50 percent discount on their bill? The wife just came from a hair saloon where she had a RMB 500 styling for only RMB 220, and the husband did a workout with a personal trainer for only half the regular price. They are part of the world of group buying.

Group buying is known in Chinese as 团购 *tuángòu*. It is very popular in China, where there is a long tradition of bargaining for goods and services. The idea of group buying is simple: a business can offer a cheaper price for a product when a large group of people are willing to buy it. So group buying is organized through Internet forums. People contact their online friends to tell them about the deal. If enough people show an interest in a product, the deal is on. The customer gets a coupon for a special discount.

Today there are hundreds of deal-of-the-day sites – Singapore holds the record in Asia with over 60 different sites. But the best known and most successful deal-of-the-day site worldwide is Groupon, which offers cut-price deals on everything from restaurants to watches and vegetables. The company started in Chicago, Illinois, in the US, in 2008 and now has over 10,000 employees. The company's name comes from "group" and "coupon."

One of Groupon's campaigns hit the headlines when its site crashed because over 100,000 users tried to buy a Starbucks' $10 gift ecard at a 50 percent discount! No saving is too small for a real bargain hunter!

B) The main idea Which sentence gives the main idea of the text? A, B, or C?

A How to find the best deal-of-the-day.
B How deal-of-the-day websites work.
C Deal-of-the-day websites in China.

C) Comprehension

1 Name three bargains the couple in Shanghai enjoyed.
2 Why is group buying so popular in China?
3 Where and when was Groupon founded?
4 What do these numbers refer to?

| 10 | 60 | 500 | 10,000 | 100,000 |

D) Now you Have you ever bought anything on a deal-of-the-day site? Tell a partner about your experience.

I can understand an article about group buying.

6 Business writing
Report on a sales trip

A Ahmad Halim is a salesperson for Choc-o-Bars. The information in his sales report is mixed up. Which information belongs to which heading? Draw lines.

Choc-o-Bars — REPORT ON SALES TRIP

Date of trip	Mr. David Chang
Name of customer/store	Presentation of our new Tasty Bar to sales staff. Advised staff to display new Tasty Bar with our new display designs.
City/country	June 24
Contact person	Send Mr. Chang 500 advertising brochures.
Activity	Taipei, Taiwan
Follow-up	Sweetie Time Store in the 101 shopping mall

B 🔊 30 Ahmad is telling a co-worker about two other sales trips. Listen and complete the sales reports.

Choc-o-Bars — REPORT ON SALES TRIP

Date of trip	July 13
Name of customer/store	Patisserie Nina
City/country	....
Contact person	Ms. Kana Sato
Activity	Ms. Sato is a new customer, so I told her about .... and ....
Follow-up	Send samples of ....

Choc-o-Bars — REPORT ON SALES TRIP

Date of trip	....
Name of customer/store	Sweet Dreams
City/country	....
Contact person	Mr. Lee Min-jun
Activity	Discussed ....
Follow-up	....

I can write a short sales report.

TOEIC® practice

1 Listening

[31] Talks You will hear a voicemail message. Choose the best answer to each question.

1 When should you call back?
- [ ] A any time from Monday to Friday
- [ ] B any day after 9 AM
- [ ] C on weekends
- [ ] D during business hours

2 If you don't want to leave a message, how can you contact the company?
- [ ] A Send an email.
- [ ] B Send a fax.
- [ ] C Write a letter.
- [ ] D Send a text message.

3 Which information does the company want from you?
- [ ] A your email address
- [ ] B your phone number
- [ ] C your home address
- [ ] D your fax number

2 Speaking

[32] Respond to questions using the information provided You will answer three questions based on the information below. You have 30 seconds to read the information before the questions begin. Respond immediately after each question.

Course dates and fees

Course type and length	Starting date	Fees incl. accommodation
Business English 1 week	July 15	US$800
General English 1 week	July 29	US$700
General English 2 weeks	August 5	US$1,350
Business English 2 weeks	August 19	US$1,550
Business English 1 week	September 2	US$800

Richmond School of English

Daily timetable Mon.–Sat.

08:30 AM – 09:00 AM	Breakfast
09:00 AM – 10:30 AM	Lessons
10:30 AM – 11:00 AM	Break
11:00 AM – 12.30 PM	Lessons
12:30 PM – 01:30 PM	Lunch
01.30 PM – 03:00 PM	Lessons
03:00 PM – 05:30 PM	Students have a choice of activities (e.g., shopping, visiting a museum, going to the movies).

Question 1
Can you offer us a two-week business English course before September?

Question 2
What does the course cost?

Question 3
What can students do after the daily lessons?

3 Reading

Reading comprehension Read the text and choose the best answer.

> Dear Deborah:
>
> Thank you for your email informing us of Mr. Brown's travel arrangements. We note that he will be flying in from Sydney on June 12 and departing on June 15. Our Marketing Director, Mr. Castillo, is looking forward to his visit and to his presentation.
>
> As you requested, I have reserved a room for Mr. Brown in the Dorada Hotel here in the center of Manila, tel. +63 (0)2 5269894. We have an English-speaking driver who will pick him up at International Arrivals and take him to the hotel. The driver will hold a sign with our company logo so that Mr. Brown can recognize him.
>
> As part of the social program, Mr. Castillo has organized a trip to the opera and a formal dinner with some important business contacts, so you might like to remind Mr. Brown to bring some suitable clothes.
>
> We wish Mr. Brown a pleasant flight.
>
> Kind regards,
>
> Patricia Garcia
> Assistant to the Marketing Director

1. Who is Patricia Garcia?
   - [ ] A a marketing director in Manila
   - [ ] B a marketing assistant in Manila
   - [ ] C Mr. Brown's personal assistant
   - [ ] D Mr. Castillo's personal assistant

2. What did Deborah ask Patricia to do?
   - [ ] A make travel arrangements
   - [ ] B book a hotel in Manila
   - [ ] C organize a pick-up service
   - [ ] D find an English-speaking driver

3. How will Mr. Brown recognize the driver?
   - [ ] A The driver will speak to him in English.
   - [ ] B The driver will wait at International Arrivals.
   - [ ] C Mr. Brown knows the company logo.
   - [ ] D Mr. Brown has met the driver before.

4. What will Mr. Brown need to bring?
   - [ ] A the address of the hotel
   - [ ] B the address of the company
   - [ ] C some opera tickets
   - [ ] D some formal clothes

4 Writing

Write a sentence based on a picture. Write ONE sentence based on each picture. You must use the two words or phrases that are given with the picture.

Example: presentation / co-workers
Possible answer:
A businesswoman is giving a presentation to her co-workers.

1 tourists / currency

2 break down / contact

Unit 7

Future trends

1 Business situation
Top jobs for the future

food chemist

environment engineer

privacy adviser

A 🎧 33 Listen to three young people talking about their career choices and check (✔) the correct answer.

Who . . .	Eva	Max	Kaito
1 is from Taiwan?	☐	☐	☐
2 is studying in Melbourne?	☐	☐	☐
3 talks about security systems?	☐	☐	☐
4 wants to work abroad?	☐	☐	☐
5 is going to leave college next year?	☐	☐	☐
6 already has a job?	☐	☐	☐
7 expects to earn a lot of money?	☐	☐	☐
8 is interested in working with astronauts?	☐	☐	☐
9 will finish studying next month?	☐	☐	☐
10 is going to work in an exciting field?	☐	☐	☐

B 🎧 33 Listen again and complete the sentences.

1 A food chemist develops and improves ……….
2 It's also the job of a food chemist to ……….
3 An environment engineer's job is to protect ……….
4 And environment engineer has to make sure that ……….
5 A privacy adviser analyzes ………. and helps you to ……….

▷ ▪ trend ▪ undergraduate ▪ to major in
▪ solar power ▪ security

I can understand people talking about their future careers.

2 Grammar focus
Will and going to future

A Look at the sentences from 1A. Are the speakers making predictions about the future or talking about plans? Write *PR* for prediction or *PL* for plan.

1 I'm going to be a food chemist. ....
2 I expect it'll be a very exciting field to work in. ....
3 I'm going to specialize in alternative energy. ....
4 I think it'll be a good job for the future. ....
5 I'm going to work here for a couple of years. ....
6 I'm going to train to be a privacy adviser. ....
7 I'm sure there'll be a lot of work for privacy advisers in future. ....
8 I'll probably make a lot of money. ....

B Complete the rule.

> When we talk about a prediction for the future, we use .... + verb.
> When we talk about a definite plan for the future, we use .... + verb.

C Yuka and Daiki have answered some questions about their future plans. Match questions 1 to 4 with an answer A to D from each of them. Which of the two has definite plans?

1 What are you going to do when you leave college?
2 Where are you going to spend your next vacation?
3 Where are you going to have lunch today?
4 What are you going to do after college today?

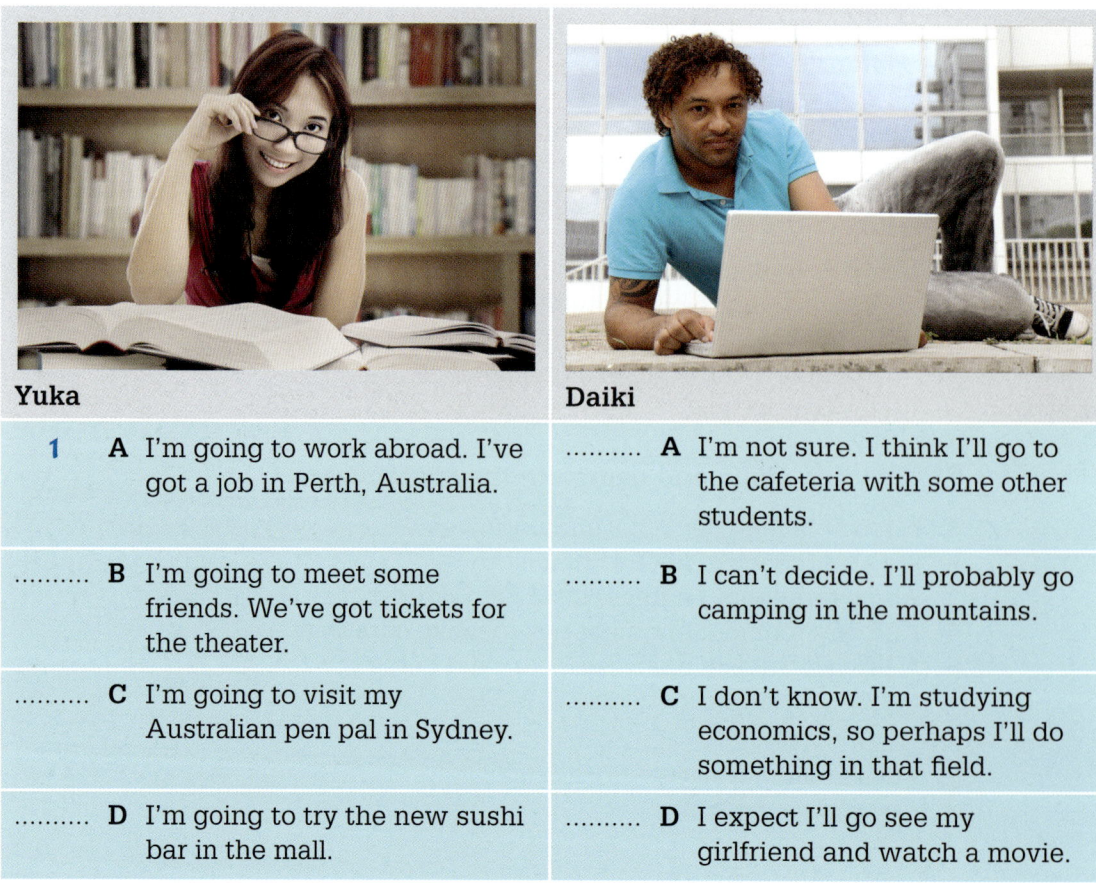

	Yuka		Daiki
1	A I'm going to work abroad. I've got a job in Perth, Australia.	....	A I'm not sure. I think I'll go to the cafeteria with some other students.
....	B I'm going to meet some friends. We've got tickets for the theater.	....	B I can't decide. I'll probably go camping in the mountains.
....	C I'm going to visit my Australian pen pal in Sydney.	....	C I don't know. I'm studying economics, so perhaps I'll do something in that field.
....	D I'm going to try the new sushi bar in the mall.	....	D I expect I'll go see my girlfriend and watch a movie.

D Work with a partner. Ask and answer the four questions in 2C about the future and ask for more information.

A: *What are you going to do when you leave college?*
B: *I'm going to look for a job.*
A: *Do you think you'll go abroad?*
B: *No, I probably won't. I want to stay here.*

E Match a sentence beginning (1–10) with an ending (A–J) and add *to*.

Eva is going to the US to improve her English.
= because she wants to improve

1 Food chemists put chemicals in food
2 I think I'll call a privacy adviser
3 I'm reading this computer magazine
4 Ly got a job
5 Yuka wants to go to Sydney
6 Daiki wants to go to the cafeteria
7 Max went to Melbourne University
8 We'll need more practice
9 I'm going to get a loan
10 Kaito turned on the computer

A visit her pen pal.
B have coffee with some other students.
C make it taste better.
D ask for advice.
E speak English really well.
F study at a university.
G study environmental engineering.
H check his emails.
I find out about the latest tablets.
J earn money for a vacation.

Food chemists put chemicals in food to make it taste better.

F Complete the text with the correct form of the verbs in brackets ( ).

Yuka is 20 years old. She's a student in Tokyo. She is studying hard **1** .... (pass) her exams. When she leaves college, she **2** .... (work) abroad and she already has a job. She **3** .... (spend) six months in Australia **4** .... (improve) her English. She **5** .... (live) with a family and look after their children. She hopes to save enough money **6** .... (travel) around Australia. She plans to go to Sydney first **7** .... (visit) her pen pal, Sandy. Sandy loves surfing and she **8** .... (teach) Yuka how to surf. Yuka hopes it **9** .... (be) a great adventure. When she's in Sydney, Yuka **10** .... (probably visit) the famous opera house **11** .... (see) one of her favorite operas.

- alternative energy - prediction
- abroad - economics

I can use will and going to to talk about the future.

3 Listening and speaking
The future of education?

A 🎧 34 Listen to Isabel Shore interviewing Tim Long about future trends in education. Check (✔) what you find out about Tim.

1. His age ☐
2. Where he lives ☐
3. His specialty ☐
4. His education ☐
5. His family ☐

B 🎧 34 Listen again and answer the questions.

1. How does Tim prepare a lesson?
2. Why is Tim going to look for experts?
3. Who were Tim's first students?
4. What gave Tim the idea for Long's Academy?
5. What makes Tim's online lessons so attractive?
6. What is the new teaching and learning method?
7. What will be missing in the classrooms of the future?
8. Tim gives four reasons why he thinks the new method will be successful. What are they?

C Work in small groups. Make a list of the advantages and disadvantages of the future schools and colleges that Tim describes. Tell the class.

D Talking about ... future trends

Step 1: Look at these predictions for the year 2030. Rank them 1 to 6.
1. definitely   3. probably   5. probably not
2. possibly   4. perhaps   6. definitely not

> **In my country by 2030, ...**
> ☐ most people will work from home.
> ☐ public transportation will be free.
> ☐ many people will take trips into space.
> ☐ most cars will be electric.
> ☐ there will be more old people than young people.
> ☐ most people will speak English.

Step 2: Discuss your answers with a partner.
Do you think most people will work from home?
No, probably not. I think some people will work from home but not most people.

Step 3: Ask your partner about his/her own future. Topics:
work in another country   move to a different city   run your own business
have children   be famous

Do you think you will work in another country one day?
Yes. I hope I'll work somewhere abroad, perhaps in Australia.

▷ ▪ education ▪ lecture
   ▪ subject ▪ feedback

I can understand and talk about future trends.

4 Vocabulary focus
Focus 1: Work and jobs

A Match the pictures with the jobs.

accountant   architect   dentist   electrician   laboratory technician
lawyer   market researcher   TV journalist

1 ....   2 ....   3 ....   4 ....

5 ....   6 ....   7 ....   8 ....

B Which of the verbs below belong to which job?

advise: *accountant, lawyer*   control: ....   install: ....
analyze: ....   design: ....   interview: ....
ask: ....   help: ....   repair: ....

C Choose words from 4A and 4B to complete the sentences.

1 An electrician .... and .... electrical things.
2 A(n) .... advises people on legal matters.
3 The TV journalist sometimes .... famous people.
4 A(n) .... designs buildings.
5 A market researcher .... questions about a product.
6 A(n) .... controls a company's finances.
7 A laboratory technician carries out tests and .... the results.
8 A(n) .... helps people who are in pain.

D What is good and bad about the jobs in 4A? Tell a partner your ideas.

A dentist is a good job because you can help people. It is a bad job because you see a lot of people in pain.

E Complete the sentences with a job ending in *-er*, *-or*, *-cian*, or *-ist*.

1 A person who works in a hospital is a d*octor*.
2 A person who works in politics is a p................
3 A ph................ is a person who takes photographs.
4 A person who plays in an orchestra is a m................
5 Someone who designs clothes is a fashion d................
6 Eva wants to be a food c................
7 A person at the head of a company is the managing d................
8 Someone who knows a lot about computers is an IT sp................
9 The first person you usually speak to in a hotel is the r................
10 A person who works in movies is an a................

I can use words for different jobs.

4 Vocabulary focus
Focus 2: College and university

F Look at the phrases from 1A.

I'm **studying** chemistry.
After I **graduate** next year, ...
I'm an **undergraduate** at Melbourne University.
I'm going to **specialize** in alternative energy.
I'm going to start work as soon as I finish my **studies**.
When I get my **degree**, ...

Which word means:

1 a university or college qualification
2 complete a course with a degree
3 a student's work at a university or college
4 a student who has not gotten a degree yet
5 give a lot of attention to a subject

G Complete the sentences with *at*, *for*, *from*, or *in* (x4).

1 Daiki is majoring .... economics.
2 Max is studying .... Melbourne University.
3 Eva will get a degree .... chemistry.
4 Next year, she'll graduate .... college.
5 Max is going to specialize .... environmental engineering.
6 Kyoto is studying .... a degree .... computer science.

H Complete the chart.

Verb	Person	Verb	Person
to advise	....	....	researcher
....	analyst	to lecture	....
to graduate	....	....	trainer, trainee
....	student	to specialize	....

I In what order do these things happen? Write numbers 1 to 6.

☐ be an undergraduate
☐ get a loan to study
☐ apply for admittance to college
☐ graduate from college
[1] graduate from high school
☐ pass final exams

J Talk about yourself.

1 What are you studying to be?
2 When did you start your course?
3 When will you graduate?
4 Is there something you want to specialize in?

K ▷ **Key words** Look at the words at the bottom of pages 55–58. Choose the best word to complete the sentences.

1 Wind energy and solar power are forms of ....
2 Math and English are my favorite ....
3 Daiki is studying ....
4 Some of the writer's .... came true, but some didn't.
5 There is a(n) .... toward smaller families.
6 Tim's online .... are very interesting.
7 It is important for young people to get a good ....
8 Tim gets a lot of positive .... from his students.

I can talk about college and university.

5 Reading
Tomorrow's cities

A) Before you read What do you expect to find in a modern city? Skim the article to see which of these things it *doesn't* talk about.

- [ ] charging stations for electric cars
- [ ] electricity system
- [ ] garbage collection service
- [ ] high-speed Wi-Fi
- [ ] open-air swimming pools
- [ ] parks
- [ ] public transportation
- [ ] skyscrapers

Asian Business Online
looks at a futuristic city in South Korea.

Songdo, located 60 kilometers southwest of Seoul, is one of the hi-tech capitals of the world. It was started in 2000 from nothing and cost US$40 billion to build. At first sight, the city seems pretty normal with offices, homes, shops, hotels, and public spaces. But its technology makes it one of the smartest cities in the world.

High-speed Wi-Fi everywhere makes it easy to send emails or watch videos while you are walking along the street. Sensors check temperatures, energy, and traffic. They can tell you personally when you can expect your bus to arrive, but they can also send warnings of any problems in the electricity or other systems. There are "TelePresence" screens in all homes, offices, and shopping malls so people can make video calls whenever they want.

There are charging stations everywhere for electric cars. Garbage is not picked up by trucks. It is transported directly from homes to underground tunnels, where some of it is used to produce renewable energy.

The city was planned around a central park and designed so that every person who lives there can walk to work in the business district. Kwon Min-suh moved here from Seoul and says her daily commute is a 15-minute walk across the park to her job as a translator. "After lunch, I walk with my colleagues in the park. When I lived in Seoul, I had to drive to see my friends. Here I can walk to visit them. It brings people closer."

B) Comprehension Find the information in the text to complete the sentences.
1. Songdo is special because ....
2. High-speed Wi-Fi everywhere makes it possible to ....
3. Sensors can give you personal information or ....
4. You don't see garbage trucks on the street because ....
5. It is easy to get to work because the city is designed so that ....

C) Scan the article and find words that mean:
1. zero
2. the way to and from work everyday
3. an area of shops and offices
4. situated
5. parks and other places where people can meet

D) Now you What do you find most interesting about Songdo? Why?

I can understand an article about a city of the future.

Unit 7 | 61

6 Culture focus
Names and titles

A 🔊35 Jane Smart works for an international company in Canada. She often goes to Asia on business. Listen and complete the sentences.

1. Two countries where the family name comes before given names are .... and ....
2. Two countries where people usually use given names are .... and ....
3. Chinese often use Western names because they are ....
4. The real meaning of *son-seng-nim* is ....
5. In Indonesia, you must address businesspeople with a title and ....
6. *Bapak* means .... and *Ibu* means ....
7. *Taan* is used in Thailand to address ....
8. The Japanese don't usually use given names except ....

B Which country is Jane visiting?

1 ....

2 ....

3 ....

4 ....

5 ....

6 ....

C Tell a partner what you know about names and titles in your country.

I can use names and titles in business in different countries.

When things go wrong

Unit 8

1 Business situation
Dealing with a complaint

A 🔊 36 Prim Chakorn works in customer service for the ChiangMai Export Company in Thailand. She receives a phone call from a customer in the UK. Listen to the conversation and choose the correct answer.

1. The delivery to Asian Gifts was
   - A ☐ late.
   - B ☐ lost.
   - C ☐ on time.

2. How many gifts are badly damaged?
   - A ☐ all
   - B ☐ a few
   - C ☐ most

3. The order number is
   - A ☐ AG230
   - B ☐ AG-230
   - C ☐ AG/230

4. How many items did Asian Gifts order?
   - A ☐ 80
   - B ☐ 40
   - C ☐ 60

5. What does Prim promise to do about the complaint?
   - A ☐ ask the packaging department to deal with it today.
   - B ☐ look into it and send Asian Gifts an email.
   - C ☐ send the items by express delivery.

6. When did the phone call probably take place?
   - A ☐ in January
   - B ☐ in May
   - C ☐ in November

B 🔊 36 Listen to the conversation again and match the sentence parts.

1 I'm afraid I have	....	A to the packaging department.
2 Could you just give me	....	B fix this for me today.
3 You didn't send us all the items	....	C a serious complaint.
4 I'll pass on your complaints	....	D the order number, please?
5 You really have to	....	E that's possible.
6 I'm not sure if	....	F we ordered.

▷ ▪ complaint ▪ item
▪ urgent ▪ inconvenience

I can understand a complaint and an apology.

2 Grammar focus

Focus 1: Second conditional

A Look at these sentences from 1A and complete the rule.

If it **wasn't** so urgent, I **wouldn't** call you.
I **would be** grateful if you **sent** the missing items immediately by express delivery.
If he **was** here, he **would solve** the problem right away.
It **would be** a terrible inconvenience for us if they **didn't arrive** before the end of the month.

> Second conditional sentences describe "unreal" situations – things that can't or probably won't happen.
> We use …… + a verb in the main clause and the …… tense in the *if*-clause.
> We sometimes use *were* instead of *was*:
> If he <u>were</u> here, he would solve the problem right away.

B Use the verbs in brackets ( ) to complete the sentences.

1. If the customer complained, we ……………… (apologize).
2. If we ……………… (not apologize), we would lose the customer.
3. My boss ……………… (not be) pleased if we lost the customer.
4. What would you do if they ……………… (cancel) the order?
5. If your prices ……………… (not be) so high, we'd place an order.
6. They ……………… (sell) more products if they advertised more.
7. If I ……………… (show) the bank my business plan, they'd give me a loan.

C Choose the correct sentence.

1. **A:** If I am you, I'll complain.
   B: If I were you, I'd complain.
2. **A:** I'd be angry if the delivery was late.
   B: I am angry if the delivery will be late.
3. **A:** If you go jogging, you'll get fit.
   B: If you go jogging, you'd get fit.
4. **A:** If it were urgent, we sent it by express delivery.
   B: We'll send it by express delivery if it's urgent.
5. **A:** If I was rich, I'd buy a big house.
   B: If I'm rich, I'll buy a big house.

My boss would be angry if I were late.

> *If it wasn't so urgent,* <u>I wouldn't call you.</u> (with comma!)
> <u>I wouldn't call you</u> *if it wasn't so urgent.* (without comma!)

D Work with a partner.

Student A: Go to Partner file 5.
Student B: Take turns to ask and answer the questions.

1. If you had a job with a high salary, what would you spend your money on and why?
2. If you had more free time, how would you spend it and why?
3. If you had the chance, which famous person would you meet? Why would you choose that person?
4. If you could work in any country in the world, where would it be? Why would you choose that country?

If I had a lot of money, . . .

• grateful • to look into sth.

I can understand and use second conditional.

2 Grammar focus
Focus 2: Adverbs that modify adjectives

E Look at the sentences from 1A. The red words are adverbs. They modify the adjectives.

A few items are badly damaged.
I'm terribly sorry.
It's extremely urgent.

Complete the rule.

> Adverbs that modify adjectives come .... the adjectives.

F Use a word from each box and complete the sentences. Use each word only once.

Adverbs		Adjectives	
absolutely	pretty	beautiful	nervous
awfully	really	damaged	nice
~~extremely~~	slightly	easy	pleased
highly	surprisingly	enormous	qualified
quite	terribly	~~interesting~~	small

1 I read an *extremely interesting* magazine yesterday.
2 Huang gave me some .... flowers for my birthday.
3 My boss is a(n) .... person.
4 Rita's car was only .... in the accident.
5 The exam was ....
6 I felt .... during the job interview.
7 The company is looking for .... staff.
8 Their company is very big – in fact, it's ....
9 My company is not very big – in fact it's ....
10 I was .... when they asked for my opinion.

They are *extremely happy*.

G Take turns to ask and answer questions. Use one of the adverbs in 2F and one of the adjectives below in your answer.

| angry | grateful | rich | pleased | sad | sorry | uncomfortable | worried |

1 What would you say to a friend who gave you some money.
   I would say, "Thanks. I'm really . . ."
2 How would you feel if a friend told you a lie?
3 How would you feel if you heard strange noises in your apartment?
4 What would you say if someone was angry with you?
5 What would it be like in a crowded bus on a hot day?
6 How would you feel if you met your teacher in the supermarket?
7 What would you think if someone had a Porsche?
8 How would you feel if you lost a friend.

I'm terribly sorry!

• extremely • slightly

> *I can* use adverbs that modify adjectives.

Unit 8 | 65

3 Listening and speaking
Making complaints

A 🔊 37 Haziq, Zikri, Jane, and Zara are colleagues in an international company in Kuala Lumpur. Listen to their conversation. Who talks about these situations? Write the name in the box.

1 ....

2 ....

3 ....

4 ....

B 🔊 37 Listen to the conversation again and complete the sentences.

1 Haziq would always complain if ....
2 Zara would always complain if ....
3 Zikri would always complain if ....
4 Jane would complain if .... this evening.

C Talking about ... making complaints

Step 1: Make a list of reasons why people complain. Think about:

| restaurants | stores | hotels | airplanes | trains | work |

Step 2: Work with a partner. Compare your lists.

Step 3: Ask your partner about a time when she/he made a complaint.
Where was she/he?
Why did she/he complain?
What did she/he say?
What was the result?

Step 4: Tell your partner's story to the class.

My partner complained . . . (when?) in/at . . . (where?) because . . . (why?). She/He said, ". . ." (what?). The result was . . . (what?).

▷ ▪ aggressive ▪ to complain
  ▪ impolite ▪ faulty

I can understand a conversation and talk about making complaints.

4 Vocabulary focus
Focus 1: Complaints and apologies

A Make a chart and put the phrases into the correct column.

I'm sorry to say this, but . . .
Sorry for the inconvenience.
I'm sorry to bother you, but . . .
I'm afraid there's a problem.
It won't happen again.
I expect an apology.
Please accept our apologies.
Excuse me if I'm out of line, but . . .
I'm afraid it was our mistake.
We're really very sorry.
I'll look into it immediately.
It seems that you forgot to . . .

Complaints	Dealing with complaints
I'm sorry to say this, but . . .	Sorry for the inconvenience.
. . .	. . .

B Work with a partner. Student A works for Asian Gifts. Student B is a customer. Follow the conversation plan. Use words and phrases from 1A and 4A.

Customer Service   Customer

Customer Service	Customer
Answer the phone.	Say who you are and that you have a complaint.
Ask about the problem.	You ordered some gifts three weeks ago. The delivery hasn't arrived.
Apologize. Ask for the order number.	The order number is AG-194.
Ask the caller to wait a moment and you will check.	Say that you are very disappointed with the company.
Ask the caller for his/her address.	Give your address.
Tell the caller you have found the problem. The order was sent to the wrong address.	Ask how that happened.
Explain that somebody in the packaging department made a mistake. Apologize again.	Ask what the company is going to do now.
Tell the caller you will send the items today by express delivery.	Say thanks and goodbye.

C Choose the correct preposition.

1 I'm afraid I have a complaint **about** / **for** the delivery.
2 I'll look **at** / **into** the complaint immediately.
3 The delivery arrived **on** / **at** time.
4 I'll wait **on** / **for** your call.
5 The manager apologized **for** / **about** the mistake.
6 We'll send the order **with** / **by** express delivery.
7 I want to know the reason **of** / **for** the mistake.

I can deal with complaints.

4 Vocabulary focus
Focus 2: Easily confused words (2)

D Complete the rule and the sentences below with *accept* or *except*.

> *To* .... is a verb. The word .... means "but not:"
> I can **accept** most of your suggestions **except** the first one.

1. Please .... our apologies.
2. The office is open every day .... Mondays.
3. I'm sorry I can't .... your invitation.
4. We hope you will .... this gift.
5. Everyone was at the meeting .... me.

E *Advice* or *advise*?

> *To* .... is a verb. The word .... is a noun:
> He **advised** me to save my money, and I took his **advice**.

I went to the bank because I wanted some **1** ....
about how to invest my money. The bank manager
2 .... me to invest it in a downtown apartment.
It was good **3** .... My apartment is now worth a lot of
money. If anyone asked me, I'd **4** .... them to do the
same as me.

F *Passed* or *past*?

> .... is a regular verb. The word .... is an adjective, noun, or preposition:
> He **passed** me on the street at a quarter **past** four.

1. This .... month has been a difficult one for our company.
2. In the ...., people didn't have computers or smartphones.
3. Prim .... on the complaint to the packaging department.
4. Lucy .... me in the street and didn't say hello.
5. Go down this street and .... the bank.

G *Fell* or *felt*?

> The past tense of the verb *to* .... is *fell*. The past tense of *to* .... is *felt*:
> I **felt** really silly when I **fell** off my bike.

I **1** .... very sorry when Din **2** .... down the stairs and
broke her leg yesterday. I **3** .... responsible because she was on
her way to my office when she **4** ....

H ▷ **Key words** Look at the words at the bottom of pages 63–66. Choose the best words to complete the sentences.

1. I'm afraid I have a serious ....
2. The order is very ...., so please send it by express delivery.
3. The opposite of *polite* is ....
4. A few .... are only .... damaged.
5. Zikri took the .... tablet back to the store.
6. We are .... sorry for the ....
7. You should be polite and not get ....
8. I would be .... if you could help me.

> *I can* use easily confused words correctly.

5 Reading
Solving problems with a smile

A Before you read What kind of things do people complain about in a hotel? Make a list. Does the article talk about things on your list?

Asian Business Online
looks at strange complaints in a hotel.

As front manager at the Sunlite Plaza Hotel in Tokyo, Akari Nakamura is often asked to solve problems. Thirty-five-year-old Akari says: "We try to make every guest feel special during their stay. But sometimes we have to deal with guests who are difficult to please. It's important to listen carefully, find out exactly what they want, stay positive, and try to solve their problems."

Akari was trained in college to understand guests' needs, but she says it is on-the-job experience that has helped her most. Above all, she says, she has learned that every complaint must be dealt with patiently and taken seriously, no matter how strange it may seem.

So what kind of strange complaints has she had? "For example," she says, "there was the angry Australian guest who wanted to move out immediately because the air-conditioner in his room made a strange noise. I sent somebody to check. We discovered that the strange noise was coming from an electric toothbrush in his own suitcase! Or there was a cell phone call from a German woman who complained that she was on the second floor and the elevator was out of order. I went to the second floor and there she was in the elevator. She kept hitting the '2' button. I said, 'Madam, you are on the second floor and you are hitting the second-floor button.' She was very embarrassed."

But Akari's favorite story is about a young woman who thought that the do-not-disturb sign on the doorknob inside her room meant that she mustn't open the door and leave the room. She phoned reception in a panic!

It is clear that Akari loves her job. But is there anything at all she would change if she could? "Nothing at all," she says. "Most guests are quite relaxed and don't complain. Good travelers understand that things might be different than the way things are back home."

B Scanning for detail Are the statements correct? If not, correct them.
1 Akari has learned more on the job than she did in college.
2 The air-conditioning in the Australian guest's room was out of order.
3 The German woman didn't know she was on the second floor.
4 There are a few things about her job that Akari would change if she could.
5 Many of the guests in the Sunlite Plaza Hotel are difficult to please.

C Comprehension
1 Which guest was angry and why?
2 Which guest was embarrassed and why?
3 Which guest was in a panic and why?

D Now you You are the manager in a hotel. What would you say to a guest who complained that . . .

1 the room is too noisy.
2 the television isn't working.
3 the bathroom is dirty.
4 some money is missing from his/her room.
5 there are no towels in the bathroom.
6 room service staff were unhelpful.

I'll see if . . .   *I'll get the . . . to . . .*   *I'll look into it and . . .*

I can understand a text about strange complaints in a hotel.

6 Business writing
Responding to a complaint

A Complete the complaint with words and phrases from the box.

| apology | complain | items | sorry to say | speak to the manager |
| store clerk | unhelpful | your staff | regular customer |

To: customerservice@compuworld.com
From: fdmiles@gmail.com
Subject: Bad service

Dear Sir or Madam:

I wish to **1** .... about the behavior of the **2** .... in your store in the Marina Square shopping mall. I wanted to buy some software yesterday, November 16. I am **3** .... that the young man in your store was very **4** .... and could not give me any information about the **5** .... I was interested in. I asked to **6** ...., but I was told he was not in the store.

I have been a **7** .... at your store for many years, so I was surprised at the bad behavior of the store clerk. Do you not train **8** .... ?

I expect an **9** ...., and I won't enter your store again until I receive one.

Sincerely,
Frank D. Miles

B Read the reply. The sentences are in the wrong order. Put them in the correct order.

☐ We are very sorry that you were not happy with the service in our store.
☐ In the meantime, please accept this $10 voucher, which you can use at any of our stores anytime during the next six months.
1 Dear Mr. Miles:
☐ All of our sales clerks are trained both in IT and in customer service.
☐ Sincerely,
☐ Thank you for your email dated November 17 complaining about the unhelpful store clerk in our store in the Marina Square shopping mall.
☐ However, we have asked the store manager to deal with the problem, and he will be in touch with you in the next few days.
☐ We apologize once again and hope you will continue to be a valued customer.
☐ Shuna Hsu,
Customer Service Manager

I can reply to a complaint email.

TOEIC® practice

1 Listening

A 🔊38 **Photographs** Listen. Then choose the sentence that best describes the photograph.

1 A ☐ B ☐ C ☐ D ☐   2 A ☐ B ☐ C ☐ D ☐

B 🔊39 **Question-Response** Listen carefully. Choose the best response to the sentence you hear.

Example: What are you going to do when you leave college?

    A ✔ I'll probably go and work abroad.
    B ☐ I leave in May.
    C ☐ I went to college for three years.

1 A ☐ B ☐ C ☐   3 A ☐ B ☐ C ☐
2 A ☐ B ☐ C ☐   4 A ☐ B ☐ C ☐

2 Speaking

A **Describe a picture** Choose one of the pictures in 1A. Look at it for 30 seconds, then describe it in your own words.

B 🔊40 **Respond to questions** In this part of the test, you will answer THREE questions. For each question you must answer immediately after the beep. You have 15 seconds to respond to questions 1 and 2 and 30 seconds to respond to question 3.

Imagine you are looking for a partner and have joined a dating agency. At the interview, one of the staff asks you some questions. You have to tell her about yourself.

Question 1
How would you describe your appearance?

Question 2
What kind of person are you?

Question 3
Tell me how you like to spend your leisure time.

3 Reading

Incomplete sentences Choose the best word(s) to complete each sentence.

1. Do you think you .... abroad after college?
   - [ ] A are going
   - [ ] B will go
   - [ ] C go
   - [ ] D to go

2. I'm going to France .... my French.
   - [ ] A A for improving
   - [ ] B improve
   - [ ] C to improve
   - [ ] D I improve

3. I would complain if the items .... damaged.
   - [ ] A were
   - [ ] B would be
   - [ ] C are
   - [ ] D was

4. I'm .... sorry. It won't happen again.
   - [ ] A highly
   - [ ] B slightly
   - [ ] C absolutely
   - [ ] D terribly

5. I .... Mr. Miles if I knew where to reach him.
   - [ ] A will call
   - [ ] B would call
   - [ ] C called
   - [ ] D call

6. Some people are worried .... the future.
   - [ ] A for
   - [ ] B to
   - [ ] C about
   - [ ] D at

4 Writing

Respond to a written request Reply to the email. Ask for at least TWO more pieces of information.

From: sfrw@outlook.com
To: New Songdo foreign resident
Subject: Welcome to Songdo

We would like to welcome you to your new home in Songdo City. Songdo is one of the high-tech capitals of the world and has many facilities that other cities don't have. You'll love it!

We know there are many things you will need to find out about your new home, so please contact us if you have any questions.

Sincerely,
Songdo Foreign Residents Welcome Committee

Unit 9

Socializing

1 Business situation
Networking

A 🔊 41 Listen to four conversations during a conference. Check (✔) if the people have met before and put (✘) if they have not.

1 Tuong and Isabel ✘
2 Ly Van Hai and Tuong ☐
3 Tuong and Mai ☐
4 Mai and Isabel ☐
5 Akamu and Nick ☐
6 Akamu and John ☐
7 Nick and John ☐
8 John and Rodrigo ☐

B 🔊 41 Listen again and check (✔) the phrases that you hear.

	Conversation:	1	2	3	4
1	May I introduce myself?	☐	☐	☐	☐
2	Good to see you again.	☐	☐	☐	☐
3	Do you know each other?	☐	☐	☐	☐
4	We must keep in touch.	☐	☐	☐	☐
5	How's business?	☐	☐	☐	☐
6	Is this your first time at the annual conference?	☐	☐	☐	☐
7	I'm hoping to make some new contacts.	☐	☐	☐	☐
8	Perhaps we can do business together.	☐	☐	☐	☐

C Work with a partner.

Student A: Go to Partner file 6.
Student B: You meet Student A for the first time at a conference. Start a conversation. Use the information below, some of the phrases from 1B, and the question *How about you?*

- Introduce yourself.
- Find out where Student A comes from and why he/she is at the conference.
- Has he/she been to the conference before?

> You are Nuri Darmadi or Yandi Tan. You come from Surabaya in Indonesia. Your company is called Choc-o-Bars. You are at the conference to give a presentation of your company's new products. You have been to the conference twice before.

▸ ▪ annual ▪ contacts

I can introduce myself and make business contacts.

2 Grammar focus

Focus 1: Reflexive pronouns and *each other*

A 🔊 41 Listen to the conversations in 1A again and fill in the missing words.

1. May I introduce .... ?
2. He taught .... Japanese.
3. She's really enjoying ....
4. What have you done to .... ?
5. Can I leave you to introduce ....
6. The guys who are standing by ....
7. Shall we help .... to the buffet?

B Complete the table.

I	myself	we	....
you (singular)	....	you (plural)	....
she / he	....	they	....

By and a reflexive pronoun means "alone": *I wrote the report by myself.*

C Complete the sentences. Use *myself*, *yourself*, etc. and one of the verbs below.

| enjoy | help | ~~introduce~~ | make | need | pay | talk |

1. Did Tuong *introduce himself* to Isabel at the conference?
2. If you want something to eat, Mai, please ....
3. You don't have to pay for me. I can .... for ....
4. Rodrigo didn't .... much about ....
5. If we work too hard, we'll .... sick.
6. Did Mai .... when she was in Bangkok?
7. You guys will .... passport photos of ....

D Look at the pictures and complete the sentences.

When Joe looked at himself and Jane looked at herself, they looked at ....
When Joe looked at Jane and Jane looked at Joe, they looked at ....

E Complete the sentences with, *ourselves*, *yourselves*, *themselves*, or *each other*.

1. We were hungry, so we helped .... to the buffet.
2. John and Rodrigo have known .... for a long time.
3. You must all be careful. Don't burn .... on the hot dishes.
4. Nick and Akamu didn't recognize ....
5. Everyone enjoyed .... at the conference.

• teach – taught • buffet

I can use reflexive pronouns and each other.

Unit 9

2 Grammar focus

Focus 2: Present perfect with *ever, yet, already*

F 🔊41 Listen to conversation 2 from 1A again. Complete the sentences and then complete the rule with *ever*, *yet*, or *already*.

1 Have you .... been to Hanoi?
2 I've .... visited Saigon, but I haven't been to Hanoi ....

> We use:
> .... to ask about what people have done before.
> .... to say that an action happened earlier.
> .... to say an action hasn't happened, but we expect it to.

G Read the script to 1A on page 111. Make sentences about the people at the conference with the present perfect and *already* or *not yet*.

1 Akamu – Manila (be)   *Akamu hasn't been to Manila yet.*
2 Isabel – Tuong (speak on the phone)
3 Isabel – Hanoi (visit)
4 Akamu – Nick (met)
5 Isabel – her presentation (give)
6 John and Rodrigo – anything from the buffet (eat)

H Complete the questions with the verbs in brackets ( ) and *ever* or *yet*.

1 .... you .... (be) to the annual conference before?

2 .... you .... (check) into your hotel .... ?

3 .... you .... (hear) that new speaker over there before? He's interesting.

4 .... you .... (give) a presentation at the annual conference?

5 .... you .... (write) your report about the last conference .... ?

6 .... you .... (have) coffee .... ? Shall I get you some?

> Use the present perfect with *before* and *never*:
> *Have we met before?*   *I've never been to Manila.*

I Work with a partner.
Student A: Go to Partner file 7.
Student B: Go to Partner file 8.

I can use the present perfect with *ever, yet,* and *already*.

3 Listening and speaking
Planning a social program

A 🔊42 Emily Jordan, from Australia, works at an international company in Kyoto. Her department is expecting some visitors from Europe. Listen to her and her team discussing plans. Who has these tasks? Write *A* for Ayaka, *R* for Riku, *D* for Daisuke, and *E* for Emily.

1 Reserve the hotel rooms. ....
2 Get prices from some restaurants. ....
3 Show the visitors around the company. ....
4 Find out prices for sightseeing tours. ....

B 🔊42 Listen to the conversation again. Fill in the visitors' schedule.

Monday afternoon	Visitors arrive
Monday evening	
Tuesday morning	
Tuesday afternoon	
Tuesday evening	
Wednesday	

C Work in groups of four. Look at the script of the conversation in 3A on page 112. Decide on your roles, then read the conversation.

D Talking about ... a social program for visitors to your company

Work in groups of four. You all work for the same company in your town or city. You are expecting visitors to your company.

	Wednesday	Thursday	Friday
Morning		09:00 AM – 12:30 PM Meetings	
Afternoon	04:00 PM Group arrives	02:00 PM – 04:00 PM Meetings	
Evening			06:00 PM Group departs

Step 1: Think about places to take visitors to in your town or city.

Step 2: In your group, decide on a social program for your visitors. Where will you take them? How will you get there? What will you show them? Where will you eat?

Step 3: Imagine the class is the group of visitors. Tell them about the social program.

▷ • to take care of • local
• to find out • sightseeing

I can plan a social program for visitors to my company.

4 Vocabulary focus
Focus 1: Phrasal verbs

A 🔊 42 Listen to the conversation in 3A again and complete the sentences with the phrasal verbs.

1. It's our job to *take care of* the European group.
2. We'll .... everyone .... to a nice restaurant.
3. If everyone ...., there'll be twelve of us.
4. Could you .... a couple of other places?
5. On Tuesday morning, we'll .... them .... the company.
6. We can .... a food court for lunch.
7. In the afternoon, they'll .... the conference.
8. On Wednesday, we'll .... the city.
9. **A:** Any idea what it would cost?
   B: No, but I can soon ....
10. I'm really .... the visit.

Nijo castle

B Match the phrasal verbs in sentences 1 to 10 from 4A with the definitions A to J.

A	see the sights	....	F	arrive, come	....
B	think about with pleasure	....	G	entertain	....
C	ask for information	....	H	get information	....
D	take someone through a place	....	I	attend, participate	....
E	visit for a short time	....	J	~~look after, be responsible for~~	1

C Check (✔) if the words go together and put (✘) if they don't.

1. look forward to
   ✔ a journey   ✘ company   ☐ Sunday   ☐ Emily
2. show up
   ☐ at college   ☐ on time   ☐ late   ☐ an office
3. take part in
   ☐ a party   ☐ a meeting   ☐ the family   ☐ a conference
4. take care of
   ☐ the children   ☐ an exam   ☐ some visitors   ☐ a vacation
5. show somebody around
   ☐ a website   ☐ a city   ☐ your company   ☐ London
6. find out
   ☐ about hotels   ☐ the lost bag   ☐ the prices   ☐ the opening hours

D Work with a partner. Take turns to talk about:

Take part in a meeting

1. something you looked forward to.
   A: *Did you look forward to anything recently?*
   B: *Yes, I really looked forward to going . . .*
2. somebody you took care of.
3. somewhere you dropped by for lunch.
4. a time when you didn't show up for an appointment.

I can use phrasal verbs.

4 Vocabulary focus
Focus 2: Polite phrases for socializing

E Match the polite phrases 1 to 10 with the replies A to J.

1 I really enjoyed your presentation.
2 Please call me Linda.
3 I'm afraid I'm not able to come.
4 I've just heard that we won the achievement award.
5 Please keep in touch.
6 It's nice to meet you personally.
7 Excuse me a moment. That's my phone.
8 I'm going on vacation next week.
9 Shall we have a drink at the bar?
10 Do you mind if I call you tomorrow?

A Congratulations! Well done!
B Oh, what a pity.
C It's kind of you to say so.
D No problem.
J Well, I hope you have a great time.
E And you must call me Mai.
I Oh, yes, I will.
H Not at all.
G It's my pleasure.
F What a good idea.

F Work in pairs.

- Student A covers the page. Student B says phrases 1 to 5 in 4E in any order and Student A gives the correct response.
- Then Student B covers the page. Student A says phrases 6 to 10 in any order and Student B gives the correct response.

G ▶ **Key words** Look at the words at the bottom of pages 73–76. Choose the best word to complete the sentences.

1 Networking is a good way to make ....
2 The past tense of "teach" is "................... "
3 Emily and her team have to .... the visitors.
4 We enjoyed the .... tour around the city.
5 The meeting is only once a year. It's an .... meeting.
6 Could you .... the train times for me, please?
7 The hotel offers a very good breakfast ....
8 First we have the national news, then the .... news and weather.

I can use polite phrases for socializing.

78 Unit 9

5 Reading
Social or antisocial networks?

A) Before you read Look at the picture. What do you think the article is about? Skim the article to see if you were right.

Asian Business Online
looks at problems with communication technology.

Phoning, texting, and social networking have become everyday ways of communicating across the globe in real time and at low cost. The first thing that millions of people do when they wake up in the morning is turn on their phone or tablet to see what happened while they were asleep.

There's no doubt that technology is useful, but just because we can use it at any time or any place, doesn't mean that it's OK to do so. "Face-to-face chatting is much more important for both private and business relationships than mobile chatting," says communications researcher Park Hye-min. She's worried that the overuse of devices could be harmful.

"First of all, people expect instant reactions and don't learn to wait for things. But even worse, they don't develop social skills," she says. "They don't learn the importance of body language in communication, and they don't learn to read the expressions on people's faces. It's unhealthy if everyone goes into their own personal world, and people no longer communicate with the family, friends, and colleagues around them."

So is it all bad news? "No, it isn't," says Hye-min. "If we use our devices sensibly, they have more advantages than disadvantages. Shy people, for example, find it easier to communicate online and real relationships might follow.

It seems that it's a question of the right balance between the number of hours we spend communicating with technical devices and the time we spend communicating with the people around us. If they don't find the right balance, people who are overactive in social networks can become antisocial in the real world.

B) The main idea Which sentence gives the main idea of the text? A, B, or C?
- **A** The dangers of communication technology are greater than the advantages.
- **B** People who use social networking usually have few real friends.
- **C** Relationships can't develop if there is no face-to-face communication.

C) Scanning for detail Find the information.
1. What is the first thing that millions of people do in the morning and why?
2. What is Park Hye-min worried about?
3. What three skills do people not learn if they don't have face-to-face communication?
4. Name one advantage of online communication that Park Hye-min talks about.
5. What can happen to people who spend too much time in social networks?

D) Now you What is the "right balance" the text talks about? Do you think you have the right balance? Why (not)?

I can understand a text about communication technology.

6 Culture focus
Gift taboos in Asia

A 🔊43 Rob Hall, from the company Asia-Pacific Business Specialists, is talking about taboo gifts in Asian countries. Listen and check (✔) the countries he talks about.

- ☐ Cambodia
- ☐ China
- ☐ Indonesia
- ☐ Japan
- ☐ Korea
- ☐ Laos
- ☐ Malaysia
- ☐ the Philippines
- ☐ Singapore
- ☐ Taiwan
- ☐ Thailand
- ☐ Vietnam

B 🔊43 Listen again. Where are the gifts 1 to 8 NOT suitable? Write the countries from 6A.

1 Japan, Korea
2 ....
3 ....
4 ....
5 ....
6 ....
7 ....
8 ....

1. four glasses
2. umbrella
3. whiskey
4. yellow paper
5. towels
6. knife
7. white paper
8. handkerchiefs

C 🔊43 Listen again. Match gifts 1 to 8 from 6B with the reasons A to H why they are unsuitable.

A It's the color of death. ....
B They can bring sad memories. ....
C They mean goodbye, perhaps for always. ....
D It is an unlucky number. ....
E It is not acceptable for religious reasons. ....
F The Chinese word sounds like "separate." ....
G The relationship will end immediately. ....
H It's the color for royalty. ....

D Talk to a partner. What gifts are suitable in your country? What gifts are unsuitable and why? Make lists, then compare your lists with another pair.

I can understand and talk about gift taboos in Asian countries.

Next on the agenda

Unit 10

1 Business situation
Organizing a meeting

A 🔊 44 Choi Ji-sook works for Bella Pacific, a cosmetics company in Seoul. Her boss, Frank Carter, wants her to organize a meeting. Listen to their conversation. Which of the two agendas below is correct?

Agenda 1

AGENDA FOR MEETING ON APRIL 30	
Chairperson: Frank Carter	
Topic: New products and sales strategies	
9:00 AM	Reception
9:30 AM	Chairperson's introduction
10:00 AM	Presentations by Bella Pacific, Stockholm
	Break
11:00 AM	Presentations by Sales and Marketing, Bella Pacific, Seoul
11:15 AM	Break
1:00 PM	Lunch
2:00 PM	Group work
2:45 PM	Break
3:00 PM	Feedback session
5:00 PM	AOB

Agenda 2

AGENDA FOR MEETING ON APRIL 30	
Chairperson: Frank Carter	
Topic: New products and sales strategies	
9:00 AM	Reception
9:30 AM	Chairperson's introduction
10:00 AM	Presentations by Sales and Marketing, Bella Pacific, Seoul
11:00 AM	Break
11:15 AM	Presentations by Bella Pacific, Stockholm
12:30 PM	Lunch
2:00 PM	Group work
3:15 PM	Break
3:30 PM	Feedback session
5:00 PM	AOB

B 🔊 44 Listen to the conversation in 1A again. Check (✔) the things Ji-sook has to do.

1. Reserve a conference room. ☐
2. Arrange for a projector, screen, and flip chart. ☐
3. Arrange for drinks for the participants. ☐
4. Organize lunch in the cafeteria. ☐
5. Reserve a table for lunch. ☐
6. Send invitations. ☐
7. Write the agenda. ☐
8. Bring a laptop. ☐

▷ agenda • chairperson • participant • to come up with

I can understand plans for a meeting.

Unit 10 | 81

2 Grammar focus
Focus 1: *May* and *might*

A 🔊 44 Listen again and fill in the missing words.
1. Room 102 .... be reserved already.
2. The traffic .... be bad.
3. It .... look impolite if we don't take our guests out to lunch.
4. We .... not be ready to start again before two.
5. That .... not be a very popular decision.

Conference room 102

B Underline the correct words to complete the rule.

> We use *may* or *might* when we want to say that something is **possible** / **probable**, but we are **sure** / **not sure** it will happen.

We can say the same thing in different ways:
We may finish by 5:30.   *We might finish by 5:30.*
Perhaps we'll finish by 5:30.   *Maybe we'll finish by 5:30.*

C Complete the sentences using *may* or *might* and one of the verbs.

1. The meeting .... for hours.
2. We .... the agenda later.
3. The participants .... late.
4. Ji-sook .... not .... able to reserve the room.
5. The equipment .... down.
6. The Swedish colleagues .... not .... the new strategy.

arrive	be	break
change	last	like

D Work with a partner. Take turns to reply to your partner's questions in different ways. Use *may*, *might*, or *maybe*.

A
1. What's the date of the conference?
2. What time will the meeting finish?
3. Where is the meeting going to take place?
4. Who is going to attend the meeting?

B
1. Where's Frank?
2. Will anyone make any suggestions?
3. What equipment is there in the room?
4. What will they discuss?

Answers to B's questions:
1. (in his office / in the cafeteria)
2. (the colleagues from Stockholm / from Seoul)
3. (flip chart / projector)
4. (new products / marketing strategies)

Answers to A's questions:
1. (June 10th / 17th)
2. (5 PM / 6 PM)
3. (room 101 / room 102)
4. (Lim Ji-min / Choi Ji-sook)

Student A: *What's the date of the conference?*
Student B: *I'm not sure. / I don't know. It might be on June 10th or maybe it's on the 17th.*

E Work with a partner. Take turns to ask and answer the questions. Answer with *I'm not sure. I may (not)* or *might (not) . . .*

1. What are your plans for the weekend?
2. What are your plans for next year?
3. What kind of job do you expect to have in the future?
4. What do you think your life will be like when you are thirty?
5. What kind of car do you think you'll have?

• strategy • AOB = any other business

I can use *may*, *might*, and *maybe*.

2 Grammar focus
Focus 2: Grammar quiz

F Can you remember the grammar from Units 1 to 10? Try this quiz. There is one point for every correct answer.

1 Mai .... the question now.
- A is understanding
- B understands
- C understood

2 .... is waiting in the reception area?
- A What
- B Why
- C Who

3 I'm responsible .... the rooms.
- A to reserve
- B for reserving
- C reservation

4 Yesterday Huang .... get up early.
- A had to
- B must
- C has to

5 English .... by millions of people.
- A are spoken
- B is spoke
- C is spoken

6 If we .... the product, we will be happy.
- A will buy
- B buy
- C bought

7 Last year, exports to the US ....
- A increased
- B has increased
- C have increased

8 Yi Ling has lived in Singapore .... four years.
- A since
- B in
- C for

9 The bank wanted .... out a lot of forms.
- A that I fill
- B me to fill
- C me filling

10 If the customer ...., we would apologize.
- A complains
- B would complain
- C complained

11 I felt .... during the job interview.
- A terribly nervous
- B terrible nervous
- C terribly nervously

12 How long have you and Min-jung known .... ?
- A yourselves
- B each other
- C you

Score

11–12 points: Very good
9–10 points: Good
7–8 points: OK
0–6 points: Practice!

Unit 10 | 83

3 Listening and speaking
Meeting styles

A 🔊45 Will Lucas works for an Australian company. Hari Atmadja works for an Indonesian company. They are talking about meetings in their countries. Check (✔) the topics do they NOT talk about.

- ☐ agendas
- ☐ planning
- ☐ business cards
- ☐ punctuality
- ☐ communication styles
- ☐ role of the chairperson
- ☐ flexibility
- ☐ small talk
- ☐ formality

B 🔊45 Listen again and match the sentences to the country.

		Indonesia	Australia
1	Meetings are usually formal.	☐	☐
2	It's best to arrive early.	☐	☐
3	Titles and qualifications are not important.	☐	☐
4	A little small talk is enough to break the ice.	☐	☐
5	It is important to get to know your business partners well.	☐	☐
6	You should avoid disagreement.	☐	☐
7	Meetings are often called on short notice.	☐	☐
8	Meetings usually start and finish on time.	☐	☐

C Talking about … organizing a meeting

Work with a partner. You both work for Bella Pacific. Your boss, Frank Carter, has asked you to organize a meeting with some co-workers about reducing costs in the company. He wants to use conference room 102.

Student A: Go to Partner file 9.
Student B: Below are details of when your co-workers are available. Student A has details of when the conference room is available. Work together to find the best time and date for the meeting. If you can't find a solution that works for everyone, find the best solution you can. Frank is the chairperson, so he must be present.

Frank Carter	Lim Ji-min	Jang Seo-yun
Monday PM	Monday AM	Wednesday AM
Wednesday AM	Tuesday AM	Thursday PM
Thursday AM	Thursday AM	Friday AM
Kang Ye-jun	**Kim Si-u**	**Cho Ju-wan**
Monday all day	Any time except	Monday AM
Thursday all day	Friday afternoon	Tuesday AM
		Thursday all day

▷ ▪ to break the ice ▪ disagreement
▪ on short notice

I can understand about meeting styles and organize a meeting.

4 Vocabulary focus
Focus 1: Prefixes

A 🔊44 Complete the sentences with the opposite of the words in brackets ( ). Listen to the conversation in 1A again and check your answers.

1. Room 101 is .... (suitable)
2. It's .... that we'll finish before five-thirty. (likely)
3. We'll start the day with a(n) .... reception. (formal)
4. It's .... to know how long it'll take. (possible)
5. It might look .... if we don't take our guests out to lunch. (polite)
6. The .... is that it takes so long. (advantage)

An informal reception

B Look at these groups of words and complete the rule.

unlikely	unlock	unpack	unsuitable
inconvenient	incorrect	inflexible	informal
impatient	impolite	impossible	improbable
disadvantage	disagree	dishonest	dislike

> These prefixes are used to make the opposite of words: un-, ..., ..., ...
> *Im-* is usually used with words that begin with the letter: ....

C Complete the sentences with words from 4B. The prefixes are given.

1. Will you un................... your suitcase as soon as you arrive at the hotel?
2. Your answer wasn't right. It was in...................
3. I can't do it. It's just im...................
4. Don't trust him. He's dis...................
5. She can't wait for five minutes. She's so im...................
6. I couldn't find the key to un................... the door.
7. He's the wrong person for the job. He's really un...................
8. The date of the meeting is very in................... for me.
9. The dis................... of the plan is that it's very expensive.
10. She won't change her plans. She's completely in...................

D Complete the list of opposites.

impatient	*patient*	inflexible	....	unfriendly	....
impolite	....	informal	....	untidy	....

Work with a partner. How would you describe yourself?

Sometimes I may be . . .

E ▷ **Key words** Look at the words at the bottom of pages 81–84. Choose the best word to complete the sentences.

1. Let's start with some small talk to ....
2. The .... must give everyone a chance to speak.
3. There was a serious .... among the ....
4. The marketing manager .... some new ideas.
5. The meeting was canceled ....
6. Frank hopes to develop a new marketing ....
7. How many items are there on the ....?
8. The last item on the agenda is usually ....

I can use prefixes to make opposites.

4 Vocabulary focus
Focus 2: Vocabulary quiz

F Can you remember the vocabulary from Units 1 to 10? Try this quiz. There is one point for every correct answer.

Part 1 Complete the sentences with the correct word.

1. C................ on the shut-down icon to close your computer.
2. Another word for a famous person is a c................
3. Yi Ling Tan gave a presentation of the sales f................
4. If you live d................, you live in the center of the city.
5. The opposite of *to lend* is *to* b................
6. Energy from the sun is called s................ energy.
7. A meeting that takes place once a year is an a................ meeting.
8. People who take part in things are the p................

Part 2 Choose the correct answer.

9. What's your boss like?
   - ☐ A He's ill.
   - ☐ B He's nice.
   - ☐ C He's Japanese.

10. On their website are some useful documents you can ....
    - ☐ A drop down.
    - ☐ B upload.
    - ☐ C download.

11. I was .... you gave him that information.
    - ☐ A surprised
    - ☐ B surprise
    - ☐ C surprising

12. If you pass your exams, it will be a great ....
    - ☐ A project.
    - ☐ B competition.
    - ☐ C achievement.

13. You often get a .... if you buy a large quantity.
    - ☐ A salary
    - ☐ B discount
    - ☐ C loan

14. Daiki is studying ....
    - ☐ A economics.
    - ☐ B economy.
    - ☐ C economic.

Part 3 Complete each sentence with one of the words from the box.

| campaign | complaint | contacts | dozen | loan | sightseeing |

15. We took our visitors on a .... tour of the city.
16. We can say *twelve* or a ....
17. The advertising .... was a great success.
18. If you need money, you can ask the bank for a ....
19. The verb is *to complain* and the noun is ....
20. We made some useful .... at the conference.

Score

18–20 points: Very good
15–17 points: Good
12–14 points: OK
0–11 points: Practice!

5 Reading
Meetings etiquette in Japan

A **Before you read** Skim the article and find an example for each of the following topics:

body language   clothes   conversation taboos   punctuality

Asian Business **Online**
looks at business meetings in Japan.

Japanese meetings etiquette is quite formal compared to Europe and the US. Here are some important *dos* and *don'ts*.

A Do arrive ten minutes early for meetings – more if the meeting is with a senior person. It's a sign of respect.

B Don't choose your own seat. Wait to be seated. There are old traditions that decide who should sit where.

C Do take a lot of notes. It is good Japanese meetings etiquette because it shows that you are interested. The Japanese take a lot of notes, and they might not let you forget what you said!

D Don't forget that exchanging business cards is a must, so carry lots of them with you!

E Do wear a dark suit – navy or black in winter and gray in summer. **Do not** wear a black suit, white shirt and black tie because that is for funerals. A dark suit is most suitable for women, too.

F Don't blow your nose in the meeting room. The Japanese think this Western habit is dirty.

G Do be polite to everyone. Remember that many people in Japan stay with their company for a long time. The junior employee who serves you green tea today may control a $50 million budget in ten years time!

H Don't pat a Japanese business partner on the back or shoulder. Touching your business partners is taboo.

I Do smile, be willing to learn, and ask a lot of questions about your business partner's company – but none about his or her private life.

B **Comprehension** Explain why you should . . .
1 arrive early for meetings.
2 not choose where you want to sit.
3 take a lot of notes.
4 take a lot of business cards with you.
5 not wear a white shirt and a black tie.
6 not blow your nose in the meeting.
7 be polite to everyone.
8 not touch your Japanese business partner.

C **Vocabulary** Find the opposites of these words in the article.

1 formal ....
2 important ....
3 early ....
4 forget ....
5 dark ....
6 suitable ....
7 polite ....
8 willing ....
9 junior ....

D **Now you** Work with a partner. Make a list of things to tell a visitor to your country about etiquette. Compare your lists in class.

I can understand an article about etiquette at meetings.

6 Business writing
Writing an agenda

A 🔊46 Listen to the conversation between Choi Ji-sook and Frank Carter about the meeting you discussed in 3C. Complete the agenda for the meeting. Use some of the information from 3C and the model agendas in 1A to help you.

AGENDA FOR MEETING ON .... *(date)* in room	
Chairperson:	
Participants:	
Topic:	
Time	**Item**
9:00 AM	Introduction by the chairperson
.... AM	Presentation by Lim Ji-min
9:45 AM	Presentation by ....
.... AM	....
.... AM	....
.... AM	....
.... AM	....
.... AM	Final comments by ....

B Complete Ji-sook's note to the co-workers who are attending the meeting.

> The meeting about .... will take place on .... in .... at ....
>
> Mr. Carter would like you to ....
>
> I attach the .... for the meeting.

C Complete Ji-sook's note to Jang Seo-yun about who can't attend the meeting with information from 6A and these words:

| attaching | information | sorry | worked | take | unable |

> The meeting will .... place on .... at .... I'm ....
> that we were .... to find a date that .... for everyone.
>
> I'm .... the agenda for your ....

I can write an agenda for a meeting.

TOEIC® practice

1 Listening

🔊 47 Conversations Listen and answer the questions.

Conversation 1

1 At the reception, the man
- ☐ A met some new people.
- ☐ B enjoyed making small talk.
- ☐ C was bored.
- ☐ D had a good time.

2 Why did the woman not go to the reception?
- ☐ A She wasn't interested.
- ☐ B She had no transportation.
- ☐ C She missed the bus.
- ☐ D She had an important appointment.

3 Will the woman go to the meeting tomorrow?
- ☐ A No, she doesn't want to.
- ☐ B Yes, definitely.
- ☐ C No, definitely not.
- ☐ D Yes, if possible.

Conversation 2

4 What does the woman want to discuss?
- ☐ A a plan for tomorrow's meeting
- ☐ B an agenda
- ☐ C reducing costs
- ☐ D lunch plans

5 Why can't the woman meet on Thursday?
- ☐ A It's short notice.
- ☐ B She's got a lot to do.
- ☐ C She's not at work.
- ☐ D Her co-worker won't be there.

6 Where will the discussion take place?
- ☐ A in the woman's office
- ☐ B in the cafeteria
- ☐ C over lunch
- ☐ D over coffee

2 Speaking

Read a text aloud You have 45 seconds to look at the text below. Then you have 45 seconds to read it aloud.

> Businesspeople spend a lot of time in meetings; in fact, some of them think they spend too much time. Some meetings take place on short notice, but usually they are planned well in advance. Most meetings are run by a chairperson. It is the chairperson's job to open and close the meeting and make sure that everyone has a chance to speak. Meetings usually have an agenda, which lists the items for discussion. The last item on the agenda is AOB, which means "any other business." This item gives the participants a chance to discuss things that nobody has discussed so far.

3 Reading

Text completion Read the passage. Choose the best word to complete each sentence.

NOTICE
To all staff

The cleaner found a watch in room 102 yesterday. If anyone **1** ....

- [ ] **A** is knowing
- [ ] **B** will know
- [ ] **C** knows
- [ ] **D** knew

who the watch **2** .... to, please report to the Lost and Found Office.

- [ ] **A** might belong
- [ ] **B** might belonging
- [ ] **C** may to belong
- [ ] **D** maybe belong

The Office will ask you some questions about **3** .... and will ask you to describe the watch.

- [ ] **A** you
- [ ] **B** itself
- [ ] **C** yourselves
- [ ] **D** yourself

4 Writing

Write a sentence based on a picture. Write ONE sentence based on each picture. You must use the two words or phrases that are given with the picture.

Example: look / herself
Possible answer: The girl is looking at herself in the mirror.

1 lucky / might

2 hairdresser / yet

Partner files

Partner file 1

Unit 2 2I

Student A: Look at the statements on this page. Your partner has four different statements. Take turns to read the statements and give each other advice. Use *should* or *shouldn't*.

1 "We want to have a videoconference, but the equipment isn't working."
2 "I have an important meeting tomorrow and I'm really nervous."
3 "I've got a headache."
4 "I find it difficult to get up in the morning."

Partner file 2

Unit 3 4C

Student A: Look at the pictures below. Take turns to ask and answer questions about the products. Your partner has to guess what your products are.

B: What is it made of?	A: It's made of plastic / glass / metal / paper.
B: Where do you normally use it?	A: I use it in the kitchen / classroom / office.
B: Which adjectives from 1A and 1B would you use to describe it?	A: It's something modern but very simple.
B: What do you use it for?	A: I use it to listen to music / make appointments / make coffee . . .

a hole punch

a glass

a shopping bag

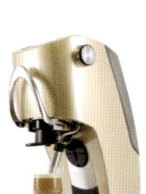
a coffee machine

an agenda

an electronic translator

Partner file 3

Unit 5   2F

Student A: Look at your profile. Answer your partner's questions.

> I'm a journalist. I work in London. I work for a newspaper called *The London Mail*. I started to work for the newspaper one year ago. Before that, I worked in Liverpool for *The Liverpool Times*. I worked there for two years and during that time I lived in Liverpool. Since I got the job with *The Mail*, I've lived in London. I live in a small apartment in the suburbs. I've lived here for only a few months. When I first came to London, I lived in a bigger apartment in the center, but it was too expensive.

Now ask your partner these questions.

What do you do?
Where do you work?
How long have you worked there?
Where did you work before?
How long did you work there?

Where do you live?
How long have you lived there?
What kind of apartment do you live in?
What kind of apartment did you live in before?
Why did you move?

Partner file 4

Unit 6   3B

Student A: Read your roles and do the role plays.

Role play 1	Role play 2
You are Australian. You have found a good job in Jakarta. You want your employer to deposit your salary into a bank account in Jakarta. Go to a bank and ask to open a new account.	**You work in a bank in Hong Kong.** An American tourist comes in. • Greet the customer. *(Good . . .)* • Find out what the customer wants. *(How can . . . ?)* • Help the customer as much as possible yourself. *(Let me see . . .)* • If necessary, send the customer to a colleague or arrange an appointment. *(You need to talk to . . .)*

Partner file 5

Unit 8   2D

Student A: Take turns to ask and answer questions.

1. If you could have any job, what would you do and why?
2. If you had the chance, what sport or leisure time activity would you try and why?
3. If you had one wish, what would you wish for and why?
4. If you had to live in another town, where would you live? Why would you choose that town?

Partner file 6

Unit 9 1C

Student A: Student B speaks to you. You have never met before. Start a conversation. Use the information and the phrases below, and the question *How about you?*

- Introduce yourself.
- Find out where Student B comes from and why he/she is at the conference.
- Has he/she been to the conference before?

> You are (*your name*). You come from (*your town and country*). You have a chain of stores called Sweet Dreams. You have come to the conference to make new contacts. You have never been to the conference before.

- We must keep in touch.
- How's business?
- Is this your first time at the annual conference?
- I'm hoping to make some new contacts.
- Perhaps we can do business together.

Partner file 7

Unit 9 2I

Answer your partner's questions. Use *already*, *yet*, *never*, or *before* in your answers.

Ask your partner questions about the photos with *ever* and these verbs: *attend*, *be*, *buy*, *drive*, *give*, *travel*, *try*, *visit*.

Have you attended a videoconference?

frogs' legs

Partner file 8

Unit 9 2I

Ask your partner questions about the photos with ever and these verbs: *attend, be, buy, drive, give, try, visit*.

Have you ever given a presentation?

Answer your partner's questions. Use *already*, *yet*, *never*, or *before* in your answers.

Partner file 9

Unit 10 3C

Student A: Below are details of when the conference room is available. Student B has details of when your co-workers are available. Work together to find the best time and date for the meeting. If you can't find a solution that works for everyone, find the best solution you can. Frank is the chairperson, so he must be present.

	Conference Room 102				
	Monday	Tuesday	Wednesday	Thursday	Friday
AM		reserved			reserved
PM	reserved	reserved	reserved		

Irregular verbs

Infinitive	Past simple	Past participle ("3rd form")
be	was/were	been
beat	beat	beaten
become	became	become
begin	began	begun
bite	bit	bitten
break	broke	broken
build	built	built
buy	bought	bought
can	could	(been able)
catch	caught	caught
choose	chose	chosen
come	came	come
cut	cut	cut
do	did	done
drive	drove	driven
eat	ate	eaten
fall	fell	fallen
feel	felt	felt
find	found	found
fly	flew	flown
get	got	got/gotten
give	gave	given
go	went	gone
grow	grew	grown
has/have	had	had
hear	heard	heard
hit	hit	hit
hurt	hurt	hurt
keep	kept	kept
know	knew	known

Infinitive	Past simple	Past participle ("3rd form")
leave	left	left
lend	lent	lent
lose	lost	lost
make	made	made
meet	met	met
put	put	put
read	read	read
ride	rode	ridden
rise	rose	risen
run	ran	run
say	said	said
see	saw	seen
sell	sold	sold
send	sent	sent
sit	sat	sat
sleep	slept	slept
speak	spoke	spoken
stand	stood	stood
swim	swam	swum
take	took	taken
teach	taught	taught
tell	told	told
think	thought	thought
throw	threw	thrown
understand	understood	understood
wake	woke	woken
wear	wore	worn
win	won	won
write	wrote	written

Transcripts

Unit 1

Track 1

Mai: Hello, David. How are you? It's nice to see you again. Welcome to our company.
David: I'm fine. It's great to see you again, too, Mai.
Mai: This is my colleague, Ly. Ly works with me in the sales department.
David: Nice to meet you, Ly.
Ly: Pleased to meet you, David. Mai has told me a lot about you. You met at the last sales conference, didn't you?
David: That's right.
Mai: Our office is on the third floor. This way, David.

Mai: Here we are. Please, have a seat, David. Would you like something to drink? Tea? Coffee?
David: Tea would be great.
Mai: How do you take your tea? With or without lemon?
David: With lemon, please. What an enormous office.
Mai: Yes, Ly and I are working on a project together at the moment, so we're sharing this big office. I'll just get the tea. I'll be back in a moment.
Ly: Where are you staying, David?
David: I'm staying at the Dragon Hotel. I usually stay there when I'm in Hanoi.
Ly: I don't know it at all. What's the place like?
David: It's simple but very comfortable. Ly, could you tell me where the restroom is, please?
Ly: Yes, of course. You turn left out of the office, go a few meters down the corridor, and it's on the left.
David: Thanks. I'll be right back.

Mai: OK, here's the tea.
David: Thanks a lot.
Ly: So what's the plan for the day, Mai?

Mai: Well, David and I are meeting Pham Dinh Huang later this morning.
David: Who's that?
Mai: Oh, sorry, he's the sales manager. We're meeting him at eleven o'clock.
Ly: When are you having lunch?
Mai: At about one o'clock.
Ly: OK. I'll see you at lunch.
Mai: OK. David, after our tea, I can show you around the building if you like.
David: Why not? I think that's a very good idea.

Track 2

Oliver: I can't believe it, Dian. It took me over two hours to get here this morning! We spent half of the time just in an enormous traffic jam. Is the traffic always like that?
Dian: I'm afraid it is, Oliver. I read somewhere that about ten million cars and motorcycles are on the streets of Jakarta every working day. And during Ramadan, it's even worse!
Oliver: Oh, what's it like then?
Dian: It's chaotic! During that month, most workers can leave their jobs early to meet family and friends. So between three and four PM it's crazy. Sometimes everything just stops, and the center of Jakarta is like one huge parking lot! Nothing moves and people get aggressive and honk their horns. Then there's the monsoon season when the heavy rain makes things even worse!
Oliver: And you live in the suburbs, a long way from the office, don't you? What's your daily commute like.
Dian: Long and stressful! It takes me about one-and-a-half hours – and that's only one way! The trip starts with an hour-long ride on a bus. I usually have to stand because the bus is full.

Oliver: Aren't there special bus lanes?

Dian: Yes, there are, but other cars often block them, and the buses can't get through. Sometimes it has its funny side. One day our bus wasn't moving. Our ticket collector jumped off and went to a bank to get some money out of the machine. She came back after about five minutes and jumped back on the bus. It had only moved about one hundred meters!

Oliver: But why doesn't the city do more to improve public transportation?

Dian: That's a very good question, Oliver. In fact, the government is spending billions on a subway and new commuter trains. But it all takes time. And in the meantime, we have to make the best of it.

Track 3

I'm **Isamu Takahashi** from Tokyo. I'm studying English and German at college. One day my German teacher invited some of her students to her home for coffee at three PM. I went there with two other students at two-thirty and rang the doorbell. We waited for a few minutes before our teacher opened the door. She looked uncomfortable, and we thought at first she wasn't going to ask us in!

Hi, I'm **Katja Falkenberg** from Berlin in Germany. Last week we had a meeting with some Japanese businesspeople. It was scheduled for two PM. Our meetings usually last for two hours. The visitors arrived punctually, we started on time, and by four PM we had discussed all the important business. Then I had to leave because I had to pick up my daughter. I explained this to the Japanese visitors, excused myself, and left. The visitors looked shocked.

I'm **Nick Brown** from England. I was working in Naples in Southern Italy last month. Now, people in Italy are really relaxed about time, especially in the south. People and trains and buses always arrive late. Well, one morning I had an appointment with an Italian customer. The appointment was for ten o'clock. Somehow I got the time wrong, and I didn't arrive at the office until ten-thirty. At first I thought it would be no problem, but the customer had left and I didn't get the order!

Hello. My name is **Anina Fisk** and I'm from Finland. I was working for a Finnish company in the Philippines a few months ago. Some of our Filipino colleagues invited us to a party one evening. They said it would start at seven o'clock. So we arrived there at seven – that's what we would do in Finland. But nothing was ready. We sat in silence while the hosts finished preparing the food!

My name is **Philipp de Woolf**. I'm from the Netherlands, and I work in Indonesia. I had to learn a lot about the way the Indonesians look at time. When I arrived, I knew nothing about "Jam karet," or "rubber time." During the first few days, I called a meeting for nine-thirty one morning. Nobody showed up until ten o'clock, and some of them came even later. I was really angry, but they didn't understand why.

Unit 2

Track 4

Sakura: Hi, Akmal. Are you coming to the videoconference this afternoon?

Akmal: I have to be there, Sakura. I'm responsible for setting up the equipment, and I'm a bit nervous about it. Remember the last time we had a videoconference? We had to stop because of technical problems – we couldn't get a picture on the screen.

Sakura: Yes, I remember. I can see why you're nervous, but I'm sure it won't happen again. Videoconferences are just so important for our work.

Akmal: Well, of course, they're perfect for keeping in touch with our business partners, but I don't really like them.

Sakura: Oh? Why not?

Akmal: Because business is about building personal relationships, about meeting people face-to-face, about—

Sakura: But – sorry for interrupting – we have business contacts all over the world. Just think of the time we would need to visit them all. And think of the cost of getting there – we can save the cost of flights and accommodations by having a videoconference.

Akmal: Yes, I know. But I look forward to meeting my contacts personally. Videoconferences are so impersonal. There's no small talk, there's nothing personal – talking about our families and things like that.

Sakura: Well, I don't agree. I'm fed up with traveling around the world for meetings! Now that we're doing more videoconferences, I can spend more time at home with my family, instead of just talking about them when I'm away!

Akmal: I know what you mean. But don't you feel shy in front of the camera? I know some people do. Me, for example.

Sakura: No, I think I'm pretty good at talking to a camera.

Akmal: You're lucky! I've got to learn to live with it, I suppose. Listen, how about meeting for coffee before the conference and you can give me some tips?

Sakura: I'd be happy to do that Akmal. See you later.

Track 5

Interviewer: OK, Ms. Sim, shall we get started? The first question is: How long do you spend online at work each day on average?

Yi Ling Sim: Oh, I spend most of my working day online in one way or another. So I guess on average about six to seven hours a day.

Interviewer: What is the main reason you go online at work? Reading and writing emails, Skyping, researching on the Internet?

Yi Ling Sim: Oh, definitely emailing. Sometimes I do Internet research for my boss. My boss uses Skype a lot, but I don't do it very often.

Interviewer: How many emails do you send and receive each day at work?

Yi Ling Sim: I guess I write between 25 and 30 emails a day on average. But I get dozens of emails. If I'm off work for a couple of days, I usually have over two hundred emails in my inbox when I get back.

Interviewer: So you don't check your work emails when you are on vacation?

Yi Ling Sim: No way!

Interviewer: What about social media? Do you use social media in your company?

Yi Ling Sim: Yes, we do.

Interviewer: And what sort of social media do you use?

Yi Ling Sim: We have intranet chat rooms, forums, and message boards, where we can post ideas or comments or upload images. That way we can discuss things with colleagues in other parts of the world.

Interviewer: Which social networking sites do you use and why?

Yi Ling Sim: At home I use Facebook and Twitter, but I don't use it at work. It's blocked. But the marketing department uses them for marketing and advertising. And my boss uses LinkedIn to keep in touch with her business contacts.

Interviewer: How do you prefer to communicate? Face-to-face, on the phone, by email or text messages?

Yi Ling Sim: Well, I like to talk to colleagues and customers face-to-face, but emails are quick, and you have it in writing.

Interviewer: Do you ever communicate with handwritten messages?

Yi Ling Sim: Not very often, but sometimes I write down telephone messages.

Interviewer: How often do the people in your office have videoconferences?

Yi Ling Sim: Well, I personally don't have them, but my boss has them a

Interviewer:	lot, and I help her to prepare for them, and I sometimes take the minutes. What about conference phone calls?
Yi Ling Sim:	My boss sometimes makes conference calls, and again I take the minutes.
Interviewer:	That's it. Those are all my questions. Thank you so much for your time.

Track 6

1

Secretary:	. . . I'm sorry, but Ms. Kondo isn't in her office. She'll be back in about an hour.
Voice:	Could you ask her to call me back, please?
Secretary:	Of course. Can she call you at the number on the display?
Voice:	No, she can call me at +81-423-45-9899 before five this evening. If not, I'll call again tomorrow morning.
Secretary:	Would you repeat the name of your company, please?
Voice:	It's the Enkai Food Company. That's E-N-K-A-I.
Secretary:	And your name again, please?
Voice:	Nobu Takahashi. T-A-K-A-H-A-S-H-I.
Secretary:	Thank you, Mr. Takahashi. I'll give her the message.

2

Secretary:	. . . I'm afraid she's in a meeting. Can I take a message?
Voice:	Yes. Would you ask her to send me a new catalog? The address is Vogelweg, that's V-O-G-E-L-W-E-G number 29. The postal code is 56068 and the town is Koblenz. K-O-B-L-E-N-Z in Germany.
Secretary:	And the name of your company again, please?
Voice:	DOMAG.
Secretary:	How do you spell that?
Voice:	D-O-M-A-G – all in capital letters.
Secretary:	Capital M-A-G. OK, thanks. And who shall I say called?
Voice:	Margarete Werner. W-E-R-N-E-R.
Secretary:	OK. I'll pass on the message as soon as Ms. Kondo comes in.
Voice:	Thank you. Goodbye.

Track 7

Message 1
This is a message for Ethan Lane from Bob Kowalski, K-O-W-A-L-S-K-I. Ethan, I'm in Singapore. I'm staying until Friday. Perhaps we can meet. I'm at the Park Hotel. The number is 065 8246 3220. I repeat 065 8246 3220. Room number 134. Can you call me today?

Message 2
Hello, this is Hendrik Edegran calling Ethan Lane from Stockholm. John Fox gave me your name and your number. He said you can recommend a shipping company in Singapore. Would you email the name of the company to me, please? The address is hendrik H-E-N-D-R-I-K dot edegran E-D-E-G-R-A-N@gmail.com. Thanks.

Message 3
Hi, Ethan. It's Ann. We have an appointment for Monday, but I'm afraid I can't make it. I'm still in Bangkok. My mother is sick, so I have to stay here. I'm really sorry. I'll call again as soon as possible to make a new appointment.

Message 4
This is a message for Ethan Lane from James Wright – that's W-R-I-G-H-T. We met at the trade show in Kuala Lumpur, and I promised to check some sales figures. You were right. Sales went up in January but fell in February by 15 percent. If you have any questions, you can call me at 0044 2456 554237. That's 0044 2456 554237. James Wright. J-A-M-E-S W-R-I-G-H-T.

Track 8

1   A   The people are having lunch.
       B   The people are having a videoconference.
       C   Four men are sitting around a table.
       D   Four people are at the theater.

2   A   The man is fixing his computer.
    B   The man is having fun with his computer.
    C   The man is working on his computer in the garden.
    D   The man is angry with his computer.

Track 9

Example: When was your last vacation?
    A   Last May.
    B   Next week.
    C   In London

1   Why are you late?
    A   I missed the bus.
    B   It's seven not eight.
    C   It wasn't me.

2   Was the exam hard?
    A   No, it was very soft.
    B   Yes, it was easy.
    C   Yes, it was difficult.

3   Is he leaving next week?
    A   Yes, he is very weak.
    B   Yes, on Tuesday.
    C   Yes, he left yesterday.

4   Is Rob taller than you?
    A   Yes, he's as tall as me.
    B   No, he's shorter.
    C   No, he's taller.

Unit 3

Track 10

Man: Can you tell me something about your latest electronic translator?
Lisa: Yes, of course. You mean the Lingua Traveler? Where did you hear about it?
Man: They talked about it on TV last night. They said one problem with using your smartphone for translations is that apps only work if you're online. And when you're traveling, you can't always get a signal.
Lisa: Exactly. The Lingua Traveler was designed *for* travelers *by* travelers. Have you used an electronic translator before?
Man: Yes, I had one a few years ago. It was quite simple but very useful. On TV they said that the modern ones are really good.
Lisa: That's right. There are lots of great new features in the Lingua Traveler. An enormous amount of data is stored on it, but it isn't difficult to use. It has a voice recorder. You can record phrases that are spoken by native speakers and practice them. So you can learn some of the language of the country you're visiting.
Man: How many languages are translated?
Lisa: Well, that depends on the model. The Lingua Traveler 01 has eight languages and the 03 model has fourteen. They all have English and Mandarin Chinese – when you think that Mandarin Chinese is spoken by over a billion people, that could be very useful!
Man: That's true!
Lisa: Old-fashioned translators had tiny screens, but the Lingua Traveler has a large LCD screen. And it has backlighting, so you can use it at night.
Man: And is there an audio translation?
Lisa: Oh, yes. Words and phrases are shown on the display and spoken aloud in the language you choose. So let's say you're in a restaurant. You can type in a phrase and show the screen to the waiter. Or he can listen to the translation.
Man: I didn't like the voice quality on my old translator.
Lisa: Yes, I know what you mean. When the first electronic translators were made, the audio quality was poor, but these days it's excellent.
Man: What happens if I spell a word wrong?
Lisa: That's no problem. The Lingua Traveler will guess the word. Now, let me tell you something about the travel features of this model. A currency converter and an alarm clock are included. It can also show time zones. It knows the time in 360 international cities!
Man: Oh, interesting. So what does this amazing device cost?
Lisa: This model, the Lingua Traveler 03, costs $199.
Man: Well, . . . I'll think about it. But thanks for the interesting information.
Lisa: You're welcome.

Track 11

Akamu: So who do you work for, Nick?
Nick: I have my own company. It's called MLTS – Manila Language Training Services.
Akamu: Really? What do you do?
Nick: Well, we offer three different services: a translating service, language courses, and cross-cultural training.
Akamu: I understand what a translating service is and what language courses are, but what is cross-cultural training?
Nick: Well, a lot of people go abroad to work these days, and it's important for them to know something about the culture they will work in.
Akamu: Um, I'm not quite sure what you mean. Can you give me an example?
Nick: Well, for example, in my country, the Philippines, we are pretty relaxed about punctuality. But the Japanese are very punctual. So if a Filipino goes to work in Japan, they have to know that, or they might have problems.
Akamu: Oh, I see. And you can do a whole course on that?
Nick: Oh, yes. There's always a lot to learn about other cultures. We talk about the way business is done in other countries and about their beliefs and customs.
Akamu: So you must have a lot of experts who work for you.
Nick: Yes,
Akamu: And how long does a course last?
Nick: A minimum of one week for cross-cultural training or a minimum of one month if it's with a language course.
Akamu: Do you teach courses yourself?
Nick: No. The courses are given by our experts. My job is to find clients.
Akamu: It sounds interesting.
Nick: Well, it's a new company, but we're doing well. Now, Akamu, tell me something about yourself. . . .

Track 12

The Association of Southeast Asian Nations, or ASEAN, was established in 1967 in Bangkok by Indonesia, Malaysia, the Philippines, Singapore, and Thailand. Today there are ten member states. Brunei joined in 1984, Vietnam in 1995, Laos and Myanmar in 1997, and Cambodia in 1999.

English is an official language in four ASEAN member states: Brunei, Malaysia, the Philippines, and Singapore. Malay is not only spoken by Malaysians but also by many Singaporeans. In Singapore and Malaysia they also speak Chinese and Tamil.

In the Philippines they not only speak English, they also speak Filipino and Spanish. In fact, there are over 150 different languages in the Philippines, but about one third of all Filipinos speak Tagalog, another name for the Filipino language.

Indonesian is the sixth most spoken language in the world. It is spoken by 23 million native speakers and by 140 million speakers as a second language.

There are 70 million speakers of Vietnamese, but not all of them live in Vietnam. Vietnamese is also spoken by Cambodians, Laotians, and Thais.

Thai is the main language in Thailand, but many Thais also speak Vietnamese or Khmer. And of course, as in all the other ASEAN member states, more and more people are learning English.

Track 13

Hi, I'm Jack, from Perth, Australia. People think that typical Australians are sporty and spend most of their time outdoors. They surf all day and drink beer all night. They greet each other with "G'day," and the men wear big hats. They have lots of barbecues and eat big steaks and kangaroo meat.
Well, that's what people think. But I'm Australian. I'm not at all sporty, I can't surf, I don't drink beer, and I'm a vegetarian. I say "Hi," not "G'Day." And I don't have a hat.

Hello, my name's Kavitha, and I'm from Dehli in India. Everyone knows something about my country – about the Taj Mahal and Bollywood films. My foreign friends tell me that Indians are poor but happy people. They are all vegetarians, do yoga, and have millions of gods. But in India if something is true, the opposite is also true! Some of the richest people in the world live in India, and yes, yoga is popular and many Buddhists are vegetarian, but many Indians are not. Oh, and my friends are always surprised that I'm not wearing a sari when I come and meet them at the airport! I don't even have one!

Hi, I'm Huang, and I live in Shanghai in China. People who have never been here think that Chinese people wear gray suits and are always very quiet and polite. But if they go to a railway station during rush hour, they'll soon see that isn't true. They think that all Chinese people are short, but just look how tall some of our basketball players are! "Basketball?" you say. Did you think that the only sport the Chinese are good at is kung fu? Wrong again. Do you also believe that rice is the favorite food of Chinese people? In fact, Chinese people in the north where I come from prefer noodles.

Unit 4

Track 14

Jack: Did you see that TV commercial for Chunky Choc Cookies, Mi-song?

Mi-song: Yes, I thought it was good. I like their slogan.

Jack: Me, too. It's really catchy. I'm sure I'll remember it.

Mi-song: Yes, you won't forget the slogan, but will you buy the product?

Jack: If I don't need it, I won't buy it.

Mi-song: But that's what advertising does to us. Advertisers tell us that if we buy their product, we'll be happy. So we buy stuff we don't need.

Jack: Don't take things so seriously. Advertising is often fun. Didn't you see that great ad for hamburgers on YouTube?

Mi-song: The one that went viral in a few days? Yes, that was really funny. But I just think companies spend too much money on advertising.

Jack: That's not true. With modern media, companies can target consumers quickly and cheaply. It's easy for them to reach billions of people through the Internet. They call it webvertising, and it's an easy way to get new customers.

Mi-song: But Internet ads are so annoying. I want to read an article. I don't want to see those silly ads for products that don't interest me.

Jack: I know what you mean. But you can delete the ads easily.

Mi-song: You seem to be a real fan of advertising, Jack.

Jack: Not all advertising. I think it's silly when a celebrity promotes something. I don't believe a product is better because somebody famous says they use it.

Mi-song: Me, neither. If I use the same makeup as a movie star, I'll look like her – that sort of thing?

Jack: Yes, it's nonsense. But I like most kinds of advertising. Billboards, for example, make cities more colorful. And I don't have a problem when companies target me through the Internet. That way I can get quick information about products that interest me.

Mi-song: Well, I really hate it when I get text messages on my phone. Last week I checked on the Internet for new sports shoes. Then I was in town, and I got a message from a sports shop about their sales campaign for sports shoes. I looked up and discovered that I was right outside that store! It feels like somebody is watching me!

Jack: Well, that's because your phone has a GPS receiver. That's modern technology. If you throw away your phone, the advertisers won't find you!

Mi-song: No! I can't live without my phone!

Track 15

1

Man: Oh, no! Crashed again! What now?
Woman: Problems with your notebook? Call Notebook City; repair and service for any brand of notebook. Our trained technicians will solve your problems. Let us help you!
Man: Right. It's time to call Notebook City's expert services.
Woman: Just click on notebookcity dot com to find your local specialist.

2

Man: Fed up at work? Ready for a break? What you need is an Up and Away adventure tour. We offer first-class tours in over twenty different countries. Let us organize your trip and we'll make it very special. That's a promise. Up and Away adventure tours. Why don't you become one of our thousands of satisfied customers? Up and Away.

3

Woman 1: Oh, dear. My vacation was great, but just look at my hair! Too much sun, sea, and sand.
Woman 2: What you need is the most exciting new shampoo on the market – new Bella Hair organic shampoo with sea minerals and plant extracts to repair damaged hair. Use new Bella Hair and your hair will be beautiful and full of life again. Washing your hair is a new experience with new Bella Hair organic shampoo.

Track 16

1 Please be quiet. I'm trying to make a phone call.
2 Our company's quite big.
3 The traffic was quite heavy this morning.
4 My boss is a quiet person.
5 Quiet!
6 You have to wait quite a long time.

Track 17

Conversation 1
Woman: Did you see that great commercial on TV yesterday? The one with the guy on the skateboard?
Man: No. I didn't watch TV yesterday. But I think I know the one you mean. It's for a sports shop, isn't it?
Woman: No, no. This one's for a Smart car. Do you have a favorite commercial?
Man: Not really. I know there are some good ones, but I don't often have time to watch them.

1 The woman talks about a commercial. For which product?
2 Which statement is correct?
3 What does the man say about commercials?

Conversation 2
Man: Can we meet at 10 o'clock. Or is 11 better for you?
Woman: No, sorry. I'll be in a meeting until midday. But I can come to your office after lunch.
Man: OK, I'll wait for you there at one o'clock, and we can have coffee.
Woman: OK. And I'll bring you a copy of the sales report.

1 When will the speakers meet?
2 Where will the speakers meet?
3 What will the woman bring with her?

Track 18

Example: What did the customer buy?
   A By tomorrow
   B A thumb drive.
   C He didn't buy it.

1 Where did you hear about it?
   A No, sorry, it isn't here
   B I saw a commercial on TV.
   C I heard about it yesterday.

2 How long will you stay?
   A Twenty-four hours a day.
   B I always stay in the same hotel.
   C About a week I expect.

3 What will you do if you like it?
   A I bought it.
   B I'll buy it.
   C It's my new bike.

4 Were you tired after the long flight?
   A Yes, so I went straight to bed.
   B No, I don't want to fight with anyone.
   C The flight will take ten hours.

Unit 5

Track 19

Hello, everybody. I hope you're all enjoying your first week with us. I was asked to give you a short presentation about the company.

First I want to tell you something about our sales figures. Last year we exported products worth 50 million US dollars to Asia, compared with 48 million the year before last. That was really good, but the figures for this year are even better. We've exported goods worth 52 million US dollars to Asia so far, and we expect the final figure for this year to be the highest in the history of the company. That's the good news.

However, while exports to Asia have increased, exports to Europe have decreased. Last year exports to Europe rose compared with the year before, and in fact we had the best figures ever. Unfortunately, there's been a financial crisis in Europe and as a result our exports there have fallen this year.

Finally, let's look at North and South America. Two years ago we opened up new markets in North America. Sales there were high in the first year, but last year exports there fell to 27 million US dollars. However, I'm happy to say that this year they have risen and already stand at 29 million US dollars. This year we have opened up new markets in South America, for example in Brazil and Argentina, but so far we have no figures.

In total, exports increased last year compared with the year before last. But this year they haven't risen. Compared with last year, they've stayed the same.

Track 20

Interviewer: Welcome to our program *I Did It My Way*. Our guest tonight is sports store owner, Sebastian Patel. Sebastian, welcome to the program.
Sebastian: Thank you. It's good to be here.
Interviewer: Sebastian, most people know you as a successful businessman. But you were a successful sportsman before that. Tell us how you started.
Sebastian: Well, my father was a great runner. In 1976, he came from India to live in London, where he met my English mother.
Interviewer: And that's where you were born, right?
Sebastian: Yes. In 1980. We lived in a really poor district of London, and we didn't have much money. Running cost nothing, so my dad and I spent our free time running through the city's parks.
Interviewer: When did you run your first race?
Sebastian: Oh, that was at school, and everybody was surprised how fast I was!
Interviewer: What happened then?
Sebastian: My gym teacher coached me.
Interviewer: And when was your first important competition?
Sebastian: When I was nineteen. I ran in my first European competition. I ran 800 meters in one minute fifty seconds.
Interviewer: Wow! And in the last five years, you have opened a chain of successful sports stores.
Sebastian: Yes.
Interviewer: And this year Sebastian, you have given half a million pounds to build a sports club in the London district where you came from. Tell us why you did that.
Sebastian: I want poor kids there to have the chance to do sports. It may be a way to a better future.
Interviewer: Thank you for talking to us, Sebastian.

Track 21

Good morning. My name is Peter Garcia. Today I'd like to tell you something about my company, Solar Light. It was founded in 2010 and is located in Manila. Solar Light produces high-quality solar panels. Our main customers are solar energy companies in Asia. Solar Light has 45 employees in the office, the factory, and in sales. We have revenue of five million US$ per year. That's all I want to tell you today. If you have any questions, please ask me.

Track 22

1 Forget it. That won't work.
2 I wish you the best of luck with your exams.
3 That's enough! Now go away and leave me alone.
4 If you want to talk, I'll be home this evening.
5 You passed your exams! Great!
6 You want to do what? That's such a crazy idea!
7 Could you speak a little louder, please?
8 I'm sorry. I can't tell you who the president of Brazil is.

Unit 6

Track 23

Conversation 1

Kasem: Good morning. My name is Kasem Wattana. How can I help you?
May Watson: My name is May Watson. I'd like to open an account.
Kasem: What kind of account would you like? A savings account or a checking account?
May Watson: Oh, I'm not sure. I've just moved here. I've found a job that starts next week, and I want my employer to deposit my salary into a bank account.
Kasem: I see. Well, most people who need an account for their salary choose a checking account. From this account, you can pay your bills by bank transfer, or get cash from an ATM.
May Watson: Yes, that's exactly what I need.
Kasem: Then may I ask you to fill out this form?

Conversation 2

Kasem: Good morning, Mr. O'Brian. What can I do for you today?
Mr. O'Brian: Mr. Wattana, you remember the business I started last year?
Kasem: Yes, of course. Souvenir Land – the shop you opened in the Riverfront shopping mall. I hear that it's going well.
Mr. O'Brian: Yes, it is. So I want to open another shop, and I'd like the bank to give me a loan. There's a shop in Siam Square which is empty. I can take it over if the bank can lend me the money.
Kasem: How much do you want to borrow, Mr. O'Brian?
Mr. O'Brian: I guess I need about a million baht.
Kasem: Mr. O'Brian, you need to talk to Ms. Mookjai. She's the person that deals with loans. I'll get her secretary to give you an appointment right away.
Mr. O'Brian: OK, she was the person I spoke to last time. She was very helpful.

Conversation 3

Tourist: Excuse me. Do you speak English?
Kasem: Yes, I do. How can I help you?
Tourist: Can you help me to change some money, please?
Kasem: Yes, of course. Is it cash or traveler's checks?
Tourist: I have US dollars traveler's checks.
Kasem: And what amount are you changing?
Tourist: The checks I have are for 100 dollars each. I'd like to change 200 dollars. What's the exchange rate?
Kasem: It's 32 baht to the dollar. Please sign the checks and take them to the desk over there. My colleague will take care of you.
Tourist: Thanks.

Track 24

Interviewer: Nuri, Yandi, so where did you get the idea for your business?

Nuri: Well, we first got the idea for Choc-o-Bars a few years ago when I read in a newspaper that chocolate sales in Asia are increasing very fast – in China, for example, chocolate sales increased by 20 percent last year!

Yandi: . . . and in Indonesia by 25 percent! I had some experience in the chocolate business, so we decided to start our own company.

Interviewer: And how did you get started?

Nuri: Well, we had some savings, but not enough to start up. So we made a business plan. Then we went to our bank and asked them to give us a loan. The manager who advised us was very helpful.

Interviewer: So what was the biggest investment?

Yandi: Our factory, of course. It's only a small factory, but the equipment was expensive. We bought some of it secondhand and managed to find some bargains.

Interviewer: That makes a lot of sense. And what are your highest costs now?

Nuri: We spend a lot of money on employees' salaries, but we've found good staff and we want them to be happy with us.

Interviewer: How do you try to control your costs?

Yandi: We ask for discounts when we buy things in large quantities. And when we need new equipment, we hunt for bargains.

Interviewer: I see. What about advertising?

Nuri: On TV, the radio, and social networking sites.

Interviewer: How do your customers pay?

Nuri: Well, many of our customers are in different countries with different currencies, so we advise them to make payments by international bank transfer.

Interviewer: And is your business making a profit?

Yandi: For the first two years we took a loss, but last year we made a small profit.

Interviewer: And what about the future?

Nuri: Well, our company is growing and sales are increasing, but we don't want to sell it. We want to stay in control.

Interviewer: Thank you for the interview, Nuri and Yandi. And good luck in the future.

Track 25

Conversation 1

A: Excuse me, I think you've given me the wrong change.

B: Sorry?

A: I think you've made a mistake. I gave you a 50-pound note and you've given me change for 20 pounds.

B: No, I don't think I did. But just a minute . . . Uh, yes, sorry. You did give me a 50-pound note. I'm very sorry. Here's the right change.

A: Thank you very much.

Conversation 2

A: I'd like to pay for the tickets with my credit card.

B: Can you give me the number.

A: 4561 5661 2938 4321

B: And what's the expiration date on your card?

A: December next year.

B: And could you give me the security code, please? It's on the back.

A: It's 321.

B: Thanks. We'll mail the tickets.

Conversation 3

A: Here's your check. I hope you enjoyed your meal.

B: Yes, it was great. Can I pay by debit card?

A: Sure. Just one moment. OK, put in your PIN number and press ENTER.

A: There you go. Here's your card and your receipt. Have a nice day.

B: Thanks. You too.

Conversation 4
A: Good morning, Ms. Lee. How can I help you?
B: Well, I transferred some money from my savings to my checking account on Friday. I checked my bank statement online today and the amount hasn't gone in yet.
A: Yes, sorry, Ms. Lee. Sometimes it takes a day or two.
B: I see. Well, that's not the main reason why I'm here. I want to invest and I'd like to know where I can get the most interest.

Track 26

won
dollar
yuan or renminbi
pound
yen
euro
ringgit
baht

Track 27

1. The Swiss chocolate company was bought for only 65 million yen.
2. The London-based company made a profit of 13 million pounds last year.
3. The Green Corn Company's revenue for this year stands at 3.5 million US dollars.
4. The average salary for bank tellers in Germany is now 2,520 euros per month.
5. At 2,950,234 yen, the new Toyota is a bargain.
6. The average price for a five-star hotel room in Bangkok has risen to 6,500 baht per night.

Track 28

1. 1,114,136 pounds
2. 2,132,987 yen
3. 32,465 euros
4. 509,643 won
5. 94,514 baht
6. 3,687,233 RMB
7. 95,953 ringgit
8. 5,123,664 US dollars

Track 29

1. 932,600,000 dollars
2. 9,000,243 won
3. 124,498 euros
4. 2,525,003 baht
5. 72,999,555 yen
6. 941,258 ringgit

Track 30

Co-worker: I didn't see you in the office last week, Ahmad. Were you on vacation?
Ahmad: No, I wasn't. I was traveling on business.
Co-worker: Lucky you! Where did you go?
Ahmad: Well, on July thirteenth, I went to Yokohama in Japan to visit a candy store named Patisserie Nina.
Co-worker: And what did you do there?
Ahmad: I spoke to the owner, Ms. Kana Sato. She's a new customer, and so I told her all about Choc-o-Bars and gave her a lot of information about our products. She was really interested, so now I'll get the marketing department to send her some samples. I hope she'll become a good customer.
Co-worker: And where did you go after that?
Ahmad: Three days later, I went to Seoul in South Korea to visit a candy store and café called Sweet Dreams. I spoke to the buyer, Mr. Lee Min-jun. They're opening two more stores, so he wanted to discuss discounts for large quantities.
Co-worker: Sounds good.
Ahmad: Yes, I just have to ask our sales manager to confirm the discounts.
Co-worker: It sounds like you had a successful trip. Well done!

Track 31

You have reached the Choc-o-Bars company. No one is available to take your call. Our business hours are Monday through Thursday from 9 AM to 6 PM and Friday from 9 AM to 5 PM. Leave a message after the beep, or contact us by email at enquiries@chocobars.com. Whether you leave a message or write to us, please remember to include the name of the products you are interested in and a phone number where we can reach you.

Track 32

Speaker: Hello, I'm looking for a business English course for one of our managers. Her English is OK, but she needs to improve it before a trip to China, where she'll meet one of our top clients to discuss an important deal. She'll leave for China on September 3rd, so her language training must be completed before then. She needs to study for at least two weeks.

Question 1 Can you offer us a two-week business English course before September?
Question 2 What does the course cost?
Question 3 What can students do after the daily lessons?

Unit 7

Track 33

My name is Eva Chen and I'm from Taiwan. I'm studying chemistry and I'm going to be a food chemist. A food chemist develops and improves the taste and quality of food. Today, food is full of chemicals to make it look better, taste better, and stay fresh longer. That's the result of the work of the food chemist. But it's also the job of a food chemist to make sure that food is safe. I'm sure that'll be even more important in the future. They say that one day, with the help of food chemists, 3D printers will produce food for astronauts! So I expect it'll be a very exciting field to work in. After I graduate next year, I'm going to spend some time in the US to improve my English.

Hi, I'm Max Anderson. I'm an undergraduate at Melbourne University in Australia. I'm majoring in environmental engineering. An environment engineer's job is to protect the natural environment. We make sure that water and air stay clean and healthy. I'm going to specialize in alternative energy – you know, wind energy and solar power. I've already done a internship and was offered a job. I'm going to start work as soon as I finish my studies next month. I think it'll be a good job for the future because people know that we need to do more to protect the environment. Later on I'll probably work abroad, but first I'm going to work here for a couple of years to get lots of work experience.

I'm Kaito Tanaka. I come from Kyoto and I'm studying computer science. When I get my degree, I'm going to train to be a privacy adviser. Never heard of it before? You will! A privacy adviser works for individuals or companies. He or she gives advice on security systems in buildings, but also on how to protect your privacy online. A privacy adviser analyzes your Internet and smartphone activities and helps you to make them safer. More and more people feel uncomfortable because so much information about them is collected. So I'm sure there will be a lot of work for privacy advisers in future – and I'll probably make a lot of money!

Track 34

Interviewer: Hello, I'm Isabel Shore and I'd like to welcome you to the program. Imagine a time when one single teacher can reach millions of students all over the world. Well, that's exactly what Tim Long is already doing on his website, Long's Academy. Tim, how does the academy function?
Tim: Well, I record a lecture and write on a digital blackboard. Then I upload the lesson to my website.
Interviewer: Do you prepare all the lessons yourself?
Tim: At the moment, I do. Math is my specialty, but as the academy grows, I'm going to look for experts to give lectures in other subjects.

Interviewer:	And how did it all start?	
Tim:	I live on the east coast and my sister lives thousands of miles away. She told me that her kids had problems with math at school, so I started to give them lessons on YouTube. Then I began to get feedback from total strangers. That's what gave me the idea for my academy.	
Interviewer:	Education for anyone anywhere?	
Tim:	Exactly.	
Interviewer:	Why are your lessons so attractive to so many people?	
Tim:	One reason is that it feels like I'm really sitting next to a person. But another important reason is that lessons are individual because everyone can work as fast or as slowly as they want.	
Interviewer:	Do you think all teaching and learning will be online in future?	
Tim:	I don't think so. There will still be schools and colleges, but they'll be different. We're already testing a new method in the United States. Students watch my videos for homework, then they come to the classroom and are given problems to check that they've understood. If they have any difficulties, the teacher helps. There are no books in the classroom and no lectures by the teacher.	
Interviewer:	What if students don't have a computer at home?	
Tim:	The colleges stay open late, so students can use the computers there.	
Interviewer:	Is this the future of education, Tim?	
Tim:	I think it is. It's flexible, it's individual, and a teacher can work with large groups. And the students love it.	
Interviewer:	Thanks for talking to us, Tim.	

Track 35

Hi, I'm Jane Smart. I work for an international company in Canada. My company often sends me to Asia on business. One important thing I had to learn is that in general Asians are not as informal as we Canadians.

In North America and Great Britain, people have a first or given name – such as Jane or John, and a last or family name – such as Smart or Smith. In formal situations we use Mr. for men or Ms. for women, so I would be Ms. Smart. In Canada we use first names most of the time, but not many Asians do that in a business situation. So let me tell you about some of the things I have discovered.

In China, the family name is always first, so if you meet Zhang Ping, Zhang is the family name and Ping is the given name. I didn't know this, and on my first visit to Beijing, I was surprised when somebody called me "Ms. Smart Jane"! Today, the Chinese often use Western names when they do business with Westerners – they are easier to pronounce.

In Korea, the family name also comes before the given name. Koreans speak to their superiors with great respect. The president of a company is addressed as Mr. President and not by his family name. Colleagues use *son-seng-nim*, which actually means "teacher," to address each other. So when I worked in Seoul, I became "Smart son-seng-nim."

In Indonesia, you must address businesspeople with a title and family name. If a person does not have a professional title such as *Doctor* or *Vice-President*, you should use *Bapak* or *Pak* for *Mr.*, and *Ibu* or *Bu* for *Ms. Bapak* actually means *father* and *Ibu* is *mother*.

In Thailand, people like to use first names, but often with the word *Khun* in front, so I became Khun Jane. For senior persons, you use *Taan* in front of their first name. So I addressed the senior employees there as Taan Bundit or Taan Sumati.

Finally, let me tell you about my visit to Kyoto. Japanese adults don't use first names except with family members. At the workplace, they are addressed by their family name and *san*. So they called me "Smart san".

Well, that's all I have to tell you today. I hope you will find my tips useful on your business travels.

Unit 8

Track 36

Prim: Good morning. ChiangMai Export Company, Prim Chakorn speaking. How can I help you?
Paul: Khun Chakorn, it's Paul Butler, from Asian Gifts in the UK.
Prim: Oh, hello, Khun Butler. How are you?
Paul: I'm fine, thanks, but I'm afraid I have a serious complaint about your last delivery of gifts.
Prim: Oh, what's the problem? I hope the delivery arrived on time.
Paul: Yes, it was on time, but unfortunately the packaging was damaged.
Prim: Oh, dear. I'm sorry to hear that. And the gifts?
Paul: I'm afraid a few items are badly damaged. I know you would replace them if we sent them back, but it's getting close to Christmas, and we need the gifts urgently.
Prim: I understand. Could you just give me the order number, please?
Paul: The number is AG hyphen, two, three, zero. But there's another problem. You didn't send us all the items we ordered.
Prim: Just a moment, yes, I have the order here. You ordered 20 each of the small wooden elephants, large wooden elephants, small red plates, and large green plates. Is that right?
Paul: That's what we ordered, but there were only 10 of each item in the boxes and three plates were broken.
Prim: Oh, dear. I'm terribly sorry about that. I'll pass on your complaints to the packaging department.
Paul: Sorry, but you really have to fix this for me today. It's extremely urgent. If it wasn't so urgent, I wouldn't call you, but we need the gifts now. I would be grateful if you sent the missing items immediately by express delivery.
Prim: I'm not sure if that's possible, Khun Butler. You see, the manager of the packaging department isn't here today. If he was here, he would solve the problem right away. But I'll see what I can do.
Paul: It would be a terrible inconvenience for us if they didn't arrive before the end of the month.
Prim: Khun Butler, I'll do my very best. Let me look into it, and I'll send you an email later today.
Paul: OK. Thanks. I'll wait for your email.

Track 37

Haziq: I don't think people complain enough. We'd get much better service if people complained more. What do you think, Jane?
Jane: Yes, you're right, Haziq. On the other hand, nobody likes people who complain about everything all the time.
Haziq: OK, but you can complain politely. You don't need to get aggressive. I would always complain if I wasn't satisfied. For example, Zara and I were in a new Italian restaurant yesterday. We waited 20 minutes before the waiter even noticed us. Then we had to ask for the menu. But after I complained, we got better service.
Jane: If that happened to me, I'd walk out! Are you a complainer, Zara?
Zara: Sometimes. For example, I'd complain if someone talked really loudly on their cell phone on the train. I think that is just so impolite!
Jane: Oh, yes! That's really annoying. I'd probably complain then, too. What about you, Zikri. Would you complain about that?
Zikri: Well, I don't think so because I'd probably be the person who is talking too loudly on his cell phone on the train!
Jane: Ah, you're one of *those* people!
Zikri: Yes, I'm afraid I am.
Jane: So when would you complain?
Zikri: I'd always complain if I bought something and it was faulty.

I bought a new tablet from a store in the mall last week. It didn't work, so I took it back and complained. Of course, they apologized and gave me a new one.

Haziq: That's what I mean. It's always worth complaining.

Jane: Of course, anyone would complain in a situation like that. But what about at work? I'd complain, for example, if our boss asked me to work late this evening.

Haziq: Would you really do that, Jane? I wonder if you'd still have a job if you did!

Track 38

1. **A** There are a lot of clouds in the sky.
   B You can see a train in the center of the picture.
   C You can see a lot of tourists in the city.
   D There are a lot of old buildings in the background.

2. **A** The people are sitting in the train.
   B The train is not very crowded.
   C Everyone is reading a newspaper.
   D One man is talking on his cell phone.

Track 39

Example: What are you going to do when you leave college?
   A I'll probably go and work abroad.
   B I leave in May.
   C I went to college for three years.

1. Would you buy a new car if you had enough money?
   A Yes, I have enough money.
   B Yes, I certainly would.
   C No, I can't buy it on Monday.

2. Chang's girlfriend is awfully nice.
   A Yes, and he's very happy with her.
   B No, I haven't met her twice.
   C Yes, she's really awful.

3. Why did the customer complain?
   A Yes, I'm afraid he missed the plane.
   B He explained the problem.
   C The radio he bought was faulty.

4. Why didn't he take a break?
   A He had too much work.
   B He didn't break it!
   C He braked because a dog ran onto the road.

Track 40

Imagine you are looking for a partner and have joined a dating agency. At the interview, one of the staff asks you some questions. You have to tell her about yourself.

Question 1 How would you describe your appearance?
Question 2 What kind of person are you?
Question 3 Tell me how you like to spend your leisure time.

Unit 9

Track 41

Conversation 1

Tuong: Excuse me, Ms. Black. We haven't met before. May I introduce myself? My name is Le Dinh Tuong.

Isabel: Ah, Mr. Le Dinh. We've spoken on the phone, but it's nice to meet you personally.

Tuong: My pleasure, Ms. Black. I enjoyed your presentation.

Isabel: Oh, please call me Isabel. By the way, I know a colleague of yours, Ly Van Hai. Do you know each other?

Tuong: I met him briefly just before he left the company.

Isabel: Oh, has he left the company?

Tuong: I heard that he taught himself Japanese and went to work in Japan . . .

Conversation 2

Tuong: Ah, there you are, Mai. Isabel, I'd like to introduce my colleague Tran Thanh Mai.

Isabel: Oh! Nice to meet you. Is this your first time at the annual conference?

Mai: Yes, it is. And I love Bangkok. It's so different from Hanoi.

Tuong: Yes, Mai's really enjoying herself.

Mai: Have you ever been to Hanoi, Ms. Black?

Isabel: No, I've already visited Saigon, but I haven't been to Hanoi yet.
Oh, excuse me a moment. That's my phone.

Conversation 3
Nick: Excuse me, aren't you Akamu Sayavong?
Akamu: Uh, yes. Have we met before?
Nick: Akamu, it's me Nick Ramos from Manila. We met at a conference in the spring.
Akamu: Yes, of course, Nick! Good to see you again. I didn't recognize you. What have you done to yourself? You look different.
Nick: Well, I have to wear glasses now. But how are you? How's business?
Akamu: Pretty good. But I'm hoping to make some new contacts while I'm here.
Nick: Come on, I'll introduce you to my business partners.

Conversation 4
Nick: John, Rodrigo, this is Akamu from Laos. Can I leave you to introduce yourselves. I need to talk to those guys who are standing by themselves over there. See you later.
John: Hi, Akamu. I'm John.
Rodrigo: Nice to meet you, Akamu. I'm Rodrigo. We're Nick's partners at Manila Language Training Services.
Akamu: I've never been to Manila.
Rodrigo: You should visit.
Akamu: I'd like to. We must keep in touch. Perhaps we can do business together.
John: Sure, it's always useful to have new contacts. Listen, you guys. I'm hungry. Shall we help ourselves to the buffet?

Track 42

Emily: OK, the visitors will arrive on Monday afternoon, and it's our job to take care of the European group and make them welcome. Ayaka, have you reserved the hotel rooms yet?
Ayaka: Yes, Emily, and they're confirmed. I've already sent you the email.
Emily: Good, thanks. Now, on Monday evening we'll have dinner together. We'll take everyone out to a nice restaurant so that we can get to know each other. Any restaurant ideas? Daisuke?
Daisuke: I think we should take them somewhere where they serve local food. Have you been to Miyako, the new kaiseki restaurant in the Higashiyama district yet?
Emily: No, I've heard about it. Isn't it expensive?
Daisuke: I don't think so. I haven't eaten there yet, but I've heard a lot about it. They do great food, and the district is interesting for visitors, too.
Emily: That sounds good. Let me see, if everyone shows up, there'll be twelve of us. Daisuke, ask them for a price for twelve. And could you check out a couple of other places?
Daisuke: Will do, Emily.
Emily: Now, on Tuesday morning, Ayaka and I will show them around the company. We can drop by a food court in the station for lunch. In the afternoon, they'll take part in the conference. By the evening they'll be tired, so they'll probably be happy to have some time to themselves. On Wednesday, we'll look around the city. Riku, you've done this before. What do you think we should show them?
Riku: Well, we could go on a sightseeing tour that takes us around the city and out to Nijo castle.
Emily: That's a good idea, Riku. Any idea what it would cost?
Riku: No, but I can soon find out.
Emily: Good idea! Well, now that we've made some plans, I'm really looking forward to the visit – especially to the socializing!

Track 43

In many countries, such as in the USA, Canada and the UK, gift giving is unusual in the business world. However, in Asian countries, giving gifts is important, but you must be careful to choose the right gift. There are some important taboos that you should know. Let me give you some examples.

In China, you should never give an umbrella as a gift. It means you want to end your friendship with a person because the Chinese word for "umbrella" is like the word for "separate."

You should also be careful with numbers and colors. In many Asian countries, including Japan and Korea, four is an unlucky number. In Malaysia, don't wrap gifts in yellow paper. That color is for royalty – you know, kings and queens. In some Asian countries, for example in Cambodia, you should never wrap your gifts in white paper. White is the color of death.

Never give hand towels as gifts in Taiwan. Here, and in some other Asian countries, towels are usually given out when somebody dies, so avoid this gift because it can bring sad memories. And don't give handkerchiefs to anyone in Vietnam. They mean you are saying good-bye and might never see each other again.

It's OK to give whisky and other forms of alcohol in Asian countries such as Vietnam and Taiwan, but it's not a good idea in Malaysia and Indonesia, where many people don't drink alcohol for religious reasons.

In many countries in the world, including China, Japan, and the United States, giving something sharp such as a knife or scissors means the relationship will be cut and will end immediately. For this reason, in the US if somebody gives us a knife, we give them some money so that we have "bought" the knife, and it is no longer a gift.

Unit 10

Track 44

Ji-sook: Good morning, Mr. Carter.
Frank: Good morning, Ji-sook. I'd like to talk about the meeting with our partners from Sweden on April 30th. You'll need to reserve a conference room.
Ji-sook: Which one? Room 101?
Frank: No, room 101 is unsuitable. It's too big. I'd like to have room 102, but it may be reserved already. Could you check it out?
Ji-sook: Shall I reserve it for the whole day?
Frank: Yes, we can start at nine, and it's unlikely that we'll finish before five-thirty, maybe even six o'clock. Now, what equipment will we need? I'm going to bring my laptop, but we need a projector and screen, and a flip chart, too. Can you take care of that?
Ji-sook: Yes, of course. I've made a note of it.
Frank: I'd like to start the day with an informal reception at nine. That gives everyone time to arrive because the traffic might be bad, and it's impossible to know how long it'll take to get here. Could you arrange for some tea and coffee?
Ji-sook: Yes, I'll do that – and some mineral water for everyone during the meeting. How many participants are there going to be?
Frank: Well, there'll be five of us from Bella Pacific, and we've invited four people from Sweden, so we need to plan for nine.
Ji-sook: OK. What do you want me to put on the agenda?
Frank: Well, the main topics are new products and our marketing strategies for next year. At nine-thirty, I want to give a short introduction. Put down 10 o'clock for presentations by the Sales and Marketing Departments. They'll last about an hour. Then a fifteen-minute break and the Swedish colleagues can give their presentations. Followed by lunch at about twelve-thirty.
Ji-sook: Are we going to have lunch in the cafeteria, or shall I reserve a table at the restaurant across the street?
Frank: Book a table, please. It might look impolite if we don't take our guests out to lunch. The

	disadvantage is that it takes so long, so we may not be ready to start again before two.
Ji-sook:	And during the afternoon?
Frank:	I'd like everyone to work in groups and come up with some new ideas. In my opinion, we need to rethink our whole marketing strategy. That might not be a very popular decision because it means a lot of work for everyone. At a quarter past three, we'll take a short break and start the feedback session at three-thirty.
Ji-sook:	Do we need to allow time for any other business?
Frank:	Yes, plan AOB for five o'clock and let's hope we get through it quickly!

Track 45

Hi, I'm Will Lucas. I'm Australian and I work in Brisbane. Meetings in Australia are usually pretty informal, but we take punctuality very seriously, so it's best to arrive fifteen minutes early. Australians don't think titles and qualifications are very important, so we don't always exchange business cards. Although we may spend a few minutes on small talk to break the ice, we Australians like to get down to business quickly. We are usually very direct in the way we communicate – some people might find us too direct because we say what we mean and we expect our business partners to do the same. We usually plan meetings a long time in advance so that people can fit them into their schedules. That's also the reason we like to start and finish on time – participants might have other appointments planned for that day, so it's only polite to stick to the schedule.

My name is Hari Atmadja. I work in Bangdung. Even though business meetings in Indonesia are usually rather formal, people often arrive late. But we expect Westerners to be on time! You should always present your business card when you are introduced to other participants. We don't usually begin the meeting immediately. People like to get to know each other well before they do business, so meetings usually start with quite a lot of small talk. We Indonesians don't like disagreement, especially in public. It's impolite. I would describe our communication style as indirect – we don't always say what we think.

Sometimes meetings are called on very short notice. I know this might be frustrating for Westerners, but that's the way we do it in Indonesia. Just as we are flexible about starting times, we are flexible about finishing times, too, and our meetings are often very long. You just have to be patient when you do business with people in Indonesia

Track 46

Ji-sook:	It seems that the best time for the meeting would be Thursday, May twelfth. Everyone except Jang Seo-yun can be there, so I've booked conference room 102 for that morning.
Frank:	Well done, Ji-sook. Let's start at 9 AM with a short introduction from me. Then I would like to hear everyone's opinions. I think it would be a good idea to give everyone fifteen minutes each to tell us their ideas. We can start with Lim Ji-min. She should begin at about nine-thirty. Then I'd like to hear from Cho Ju-wan followed by Kim Si-u and Kang Ye-jun.
Ji-sook:	Will we take a break?
Frank:	Oh, yes. We can let everyone speak, then we can take a thirty-minute break. After the break, we can have a feedback session and discuss everyone's ideas.
Ji-sook:	I've booked the room until 1 PM.
Frank:	Fine. That gives us enough time to have a discussion and for me to make final comments. I need about a quarter of an hour for that. OK?
Ji-sook:	Fine. I've made a note.
Frank:	Could you send a note to everyone with the agenda and ask them to prepare a short, informal presentation of their ideas?
Ji-sook:	Yes, I'll do that right now, Mr. Carter.

Track 47

Conversation 1

Man: I didn't see you at the reception yesterday. Were you sick?

Woman: I planned to go. I ordered a taxi but it didn't show up, and then it was too late to take the bus. Was it interesting?

Man: No, there was too much small talk for my taste, and it was pretty boring.

Woman: Did you make any new contacts?

Man: I'm afraid not. It was the same faces as usual.

Woman: That's too bad. By the way, I'm not sure if I can come to the meeting tomorrow either. I'd like to, but I have an important appointment, and I might not be back in time. If I'm back early, of course I'll look in.

Conversation 2

Woman: I'd like to discuss the agenda for the meeting next week, the one about reducing costs. Shall we talk about it over lunch in the cafeteria tomorrow?

Man: Oh, that's rather short notice. I've got a lot to do tomorrow. What about Thursday?

Woman: Sorry, I can't. That's the one day this week that I'm not at work.

Man: Well, I can manage Friday, but not for lunch. Why don't you come to my office at ten and we can have coffee together.

Woman: Perfect. I'll ask Jack to be there, too.

Credits

The publisher would like to thank the following for permission to reproduce photographs and illustrations (key: left to right, top to bottom):

p. 1, XiXinXing/XiXinXIng/Thinkstock; p. 2, ©iStockphoto.com/SENKRON, www.CartoonStock.com/Tim Cordell; p. 4, Kristian Cabanis / age fotostock/ SuperStock; p. 5, Dave & Les Jacobs/Blend Images/Thinkstock, ©iStockphoto.com/sshepard; p. 6, ©iStockphoto.com/SENKRON; p. 7, XiXinXing/XiXinXing/Thinkstock, Tomasz Wyszolmirski/iStock/Thinkstock; p. 8, ©iStockphoto.com/real444; p. 9, ©iStockphoto.com/OJO_Images, p. 10, Shutterstock/antb, ©iStockphoto.com/SENKRON; p. 11, Shutterstock/BeaB, Shutterstock/Creativa, ©iStockphoto.com/SENKRON; p. 12, Shutterstock/Creativa; p. 13, ©iStockphoto.com/ewg3D, ©iStockphoto.com/dvarg, ©iStockphoto.com/cris180, Shutterstock/Nordling, Shutterstock/Ioannis Ioannou, ©iStockphoto.com/Samarskaya, ©iStockphoto.com/Daft_Lion_Studio, ©iStockphoto.com/Aleksej, Shutterstock/Julia Ivantsova, © Stephen Barnes/Technology / Alamy, ©iStockphoto.com/vetkit; p. 15, Shutterstock/Dragon Images; p. 17, Shutterstock/AVAVA, Shutterstock/Minerva Studio; p. 18, Shutterstock/Yentafern, Shutterstock/spirit of america, Shutterstock/Thomas La Mela; p. 19, Shutterstock/Odua Images, © maximimages.com / Alamy; p. 20, ©iStockphoto.com/SENKRON, Shutterstock/kuma, Shutterstock/v33sean; p.21, ©iStockphoto.com/SENKRON, ©iStockphoto.com/LuMaxArt; p. 22, Shutterstock/XiXinXing, Shutterstock/Bildagentur Zoonar GmbH; p. 23, ©iStockphoto.com/SENKRON, Shutterstock/Tatiana Popova, Shutterstock/Matee Nuserm, Shutterstock/Fotocrisis, Shutterstock/Ingvar Bjork, Shutterstock/Kitch Bain; p. 25, © Ira Berger / Alamy; p. 26, ©iStockphoto.com/ChrisGorgio, Shutterstock/ostill, Shutterstock/SnowWhiteimages, Shutterstock/wong yu liang; p. 27, ©iStockphoto.com/LifesizeImages, Shutterstock/patpitchaya; p. 28, www.CartoonStock.com/Jerry King, ©iStockphoto.com/SENKRON; p. 29, ©iStockphoto.com/SENKRON, Shutterstock/Gemenacom; p. 30, Shutterstock/Tsian, Shutterstock/Rafal Olechowski; p. 31, Shutterstock/Sean Pavone, © Inmagine / Alamy; p. 32, ©iStockphoto.com/SENKRON; p. 33, XiXinXing / Superstock, Jetta Productions / Blend Images / Superstock; p. 34, Shutterstock/bannosuke, Shutterstock/Pablo Calvog; p. 35, Shutterstock/Luc Ubaghs; p. 37, Shutterstock/Creativa, ©iStockphoto.com/SENKRON; p. 38, © Stuart Miles / Alamy, ©iStockphoto.com/SENKRON; p. 39, ©iStockphoto.com/waiwai08, ©iStockphoto.com/SENKRON; p. 40, age fotostock / SuperStock; p. 41, ©iStockphoto.com/bedo, ©iStockphoto.com/kledge, ©iStockphoto.com/bedo, ©iStockphoto.com/SENKRON; p. 42, ©iStockphoto.com/gerenme; p. 43, Copyright © START TODAY CO.,LTD., Copyright © Haan Corporation 2014-2023; p. 44, ©iStockphoto.com/CareyHope, ©iStockphoto.com/Yuri_Arcurs, Shutterstock/PathDoc, ©iStockphoto.com/stocknroll, Shutterstock/Malyugin, Shutterstock/Rommel Canlas, Shutterstock/Csaba Vanyi, ©iStockphoto.com/PIKSEL; p. 45, Shutterstock/Sidarta, Shutterstock/Dragon Images; p. 46, ©iStockphoto.com/SENKRON, Shutterstock/Karramba Production, Shutterstock/Andrey Burmakin, Shutterstock/Stephen Coburn, Shutterstock/auremar, Shutterstock/Lisa F.Young; p. 47, ©iStockphoto.com/SENKRON, ©iStockphoto.com/ChristopherBernard; p. 48, Shutterstock/OtnaYdur, Shutterstock/Shahril KHMD; p. 49, Shutterstock/Andy Dean Photographer, Shutterstock/Andresr, ©iStockphoto.com/YinYang, ©iStockphoto.com/IS_ImageSource, ©iStockphoto.com/SENKRON; p. 51, Shutterstock/Annette Shaff; p. 52, Shutterstock/Andrei Kuzmik, Shutterstock/Sean Pavone; p. 53, Shutterstock/Cienpies Design; p. 54, Shutterstock/Andresr, ©iStockphoto.com/robyvannucci, Shutterstock/CandyBox Images; p. 55, Shutterstock/Darren Baker, Shutterstock/Goodluz, Shutterstock/zhu difeng; p.56, Shutterstock/Creativa, Shutterstock/Goodluz; p. 57, ©iStockphoto.com/SENKRON, Shutterstock/Creativa; p.58, © Blend Images / Alamy; p. 59, ©iStockphoto.com/sturti, Shutterstock/Wolfgang Zwanzger, Shutterstock/auremar, Shutterstock/Oleg Dubas, Shutterstock/Creativa, Shutterstock/Dmitri Mihhailov, ©iStockphoto.com/OSTILL, Shutterstock/Armin Sestic; p. 60, Shutterstock/szefei; p. 61, CHASUNG YUN/iStock/Thinkstock; p. 62, Shutterstock/B. Franklin; p. 63, ©iStockphoto.com/dejanristovski, Shutterstock/wavebreakmedia; p. 64, ©iStockphoto.com/SENKRON, © PHOVOIR / Alamy, ©iStockphoto.com/williv; p. 65, Shutterstock/Phil Date; p. 67, Shutterstock/Rido, Shutterstock/sunabesyou; p. 68, ©iStockphoto.com/pagadesign, ©iStockphoto.com/stuartbur, ©iStockphoto.com/onurdongel, ©iStockphoto.com/xyno; p. 69, Shutterstock/erwinova; p. 70, Shutterstock/pcruciatti; p. 71, Shutterstock/Zhukov Oleg, Shutterstock/bikeriderlondon; p. 73, Shutterstock/Ruta Production, Shutterstock/EDHAR; p. 74, ©iStockphoto.com/SENKRON; p. 75, ©iStockphoto.com/SENKRON; p. 76, Shutterstock/Dragon Images; p. 77, Prisma / SuperStock, Shutterstock/Vitchanan Photography; p. 78, ©iStockphoto.com/Neustockimages; p. 79, Shutterstock/Dragon Images; p. 80, © East Fence Images / Alamy, ©iStockphoto.com/Difydave, Shutterstock/2happy, ©iStockphoto.com/evemilla, ©iStockphoto.com/kaisphoto, Shutterstock/Mega Pixel, Shutterstock/Volodymyr Krasyuk, Shutterstock/VladislavGudovskiy, Shutterstock/Renewer; p. 81, ©iStockphoto.com/OJO_Images; p. 82, Shutterstock/Yentafern, ©iStockphoto.com/SENKRON; p.83, Shutterstock/Lan Images; p. 84, Shutterstock/filipw, Shutterstock/Kedofoto, www.CartoonStock.com/Dan Reynolds; p. 85, Shutterstock/Christine Langer-Pueschel; p. 86, Shutterstock/rnl; p. 87, Pixtal / SuperStock; p. 88, Shutterstock/iQoncept; p. 90, Shutterstock/AVAVA, Monkey Business Images/Monday Business/Thinkstock, Shutterstock/Tyler Olson; p. 91, Shutterstock/donatas1205, Shutterstock/Wolna, Shutterstock/Daniela Pelazza, Shutterstock/Levent Konuk, Shutterstock/Dan Kosmayer, © maximimages.com / Alamy; p. 93, Shutterstock/Andrey_Popov, ©iStockphoto.com/Alija, Shutterstock/Amy Johansson, © Photocuisine / Alamy; p. 94, Shutterstock/XiXinXing, Shutterstock/Konstantin Sutyagin, Shutterstock/Darren Brode, © National Geographic Image Collection / Alamy

Cover Photo: Pixtal / SuperStock